Where Do I Start? A School Library Handbook

D1560327

Santa Clara County Office of Education, Library Services

Linworth Publishing, Inc.
Worthington, Ohio

Library of Congress Cataloging-in-Publication Data

Where do I start? : a school library handbook / Santa Clara County Office of Education.
    p. cm.
  Includes bibliographical references and index.
  ISBN 1-58683-043-0
   1. School libraries--United States--Administration--Handbooks, manuals, etc. 2.
Instructional materials centers--United States--Administration--Handbooks, manuals,
etc. I. Santa Clara County (Calif.). Office of Education.

  Z675.S3 W6 2001
  025.1'978--dc21
2001032674

Published by Linworth Publishing, Inc.
480 East Wilson Bridge Road, Suite L
Worthington, Ohio 43085

Copyright © 2001 by Linworth Publishing, Inc.

Series Information:
    From The Professional Growth Series

ISBN 1-58683-043-0

5 4 3 2

TABLE OF CONTENTS

ACKNOWLEDGMENTS

This Handbook was created by the Library Services Staff of the Santa Clara County Office of Education.

Authors: Susan Martimo Choi, Manager
                  Donna Wheelehan, Library Technical Specialist
                  Patty Beers, Library Resource Specialist

Support staff: Theresa Martinez, Senior Staff Secretary

Contributors: Alice Bethke, Santa Clara Unified School District
                  Doris Dillon, San Jose Unified School District

INTRODUCTION

"I was handed the key to the library and pointed in the direction of the library. That was the extent of the training I got when I started."

Library Clerk

Many times new library staff members would come to our Professional Library asking for help in running their school library. Often they had little or no library training and there was no one at their school site or in their district to help them.

The Library Services staff developed library training workshops including a four-day Basic Training Workshop for School Library Clerks, K-8. This workshop was designed to provide an overview of many of the areas that a library clerk or paraprofessional would encounter in an elementary school library. As we developed materials for this workshop we began to envision a school library handbook that would be useful to anyone working in school libraries including experienced clerks, volunteers and even professional school library staff.

Where Do I Start? A School Library Handbook provides a quick overview and reference for many library related topics in an easy-to-read style. It brings a great deal of information together in one document with an extensive index and selected resources that the authors have found useful. The *School Library Handbook* can serve as your first reference source. It will give you an overview and brief information on a topic and lead you to other resources for more in-depth information.

• Library Overview includes information on the mission of the school library, staffing, and policies including selection and challenge policies.

• Library Space starts with some basic principles of organization for your library and then presents a few safety considerations and concludes with an extensive chapter on library environment including displays, merchandising and bulletin boards.

• PR/Marketing will start you thinking about how you communicate with others. It includes statistics and research findings that you might use as you communicate about the value of the library with the various customers that your library serves.

• Library Collection covers the collection development process including weeding and selection of materials and includes some helpful forms that you can adapt to your library.

• Library Program provides information on booktalking, storytelling and teaching information skills. It includes a brief overview of the national Information Literacy Standards and two research models: Big6™ and FLIPit™

- Internet includes a brief overview on the Internet, some issues related to Internet filters and a bibliography of useful library-related Internet web sites. Information on online searching and the use of Boolean operators is also provided.

- Library Procedures provides general information on budgets, purchasing, receiving, processing and circulating materials as well as sample forms that you might adapt for your library. Specific procedures in these areas vary from district to district depending upon your local policies. A summary of the filing rules is also included.

- Library Automation gives general considerations when selecting an automation system. The system you use will have its own specific procedures that you will need to follow. A sample MARC record is also included with a brief overview.

The Appendix includes a Glossary that explains 200 terms used in school libraries and the field of education. A detailed index will help you locate the specific information you need. Additional resources are listed in bibliographies located at the end of each chapter. These resources are also listed in the Index by title and by author.

The authors and publisher are very much interested in knowing how you are using this *School Library Handbook* and would like to receive your suggestions for improvement. A Feedback Form is included at the end of this book. Please complete this form and return it to help us improve future editions of the Handbook.

LIBRARY MISSION

Information Power: Building Partnerships for Learning (1998), the national school library guidelines, states:

> *"The mission of the library media program is to ensure that students and staff are effective users of ideas and information.*
>
> *This mission is accomplished:*
> - *by providing intellectual and physical access to materials in all formats;*
> - *by providing instruction to foster competence and stimulate interest in reading, viewing, and using information and ideas;*
> - *by working with other educators to design learning strategies to meet the needs of individual students."* (page 6)

A mission statement is a brief, clear statement of the reasons for an organization's existence, its purpose or function, its customer base and the methods through which it fulfills its purpose. You can see from the statement above that the customers of the library media program are "students and staff" and the purpose of the library media program is to be sure that these customers are "effective users of ideas and information." The last three statements explain how this will be done.

Knowing the purpose of the school library and having a mission statement can help you to keep your focus on what is most important in the library. Posting the library's mission statement can serve as a reminder to the staff and administration about the valuable role of the library media program.

Here are a few sample mission statements that show a variety of formats and content:

- The mission of the Library Media Program is to assist students in the development of the skills necessary for independent lifelong learning. Emphasis is placed on the appreciation and enjoyment of literature and the motivation of reading for pleasure as well as for information.

- The mission of the Library Media Technology Program is to encourage students and adults to become independent learners by providing: facilities that function as information centers of the schools; resources, activities, and instruction in the use of information technology; and an environment which encourages reading for pleasure.

- The Media Program must ensure that students and staff are effective users of ideas and information to develop lifelong learning skills. The media program shall provide a structure of student learning activities with repeated opportunities in all curriculum to develop and integrate information/research skills. These skills include locating, interpreting, analyzing, synthesizing, evaluating and utilizing data from a variety of resources.

- The mission of the Library Media Program is to stimulate the power of knowledge within each student by strengthening the relationship between the student and the challenges of an ever-changing world through libraries.

  To support this mission the library media program will:
  - increase access to provide excellence in library media center resources, facilities, and services;

  - impact the instructional program for students by strengthening the teaching/learning process through staff development, curriculum, integration, and information literacy;

  - build within the community connections among school library media centers, public libraries, and other resources of information;

  - stimulate student, parent, school, and community partnerships;

  - celebrate the diversity and uniqueness of all people;

  - emphasize the love of reading and learning.

- The High School Library is committed to intellectual freedom and supports free access to information. The primary goals of the library program are to provide the leadership, personnel, resources, equipment, and facilities needed to help students and teachers to become effective users of ideas and information.

RESOURCES

American Association of School Librarians and Association for Educational Communications and Technology, *Information Power: Building Partnerships for Learning.* Chicago, IL: American Library Association, 1998.

LIBRARY STAFFING

Some states have required minimum levels of staffing for school libraries, but many states do not have specific requirements. The level and type of staffing in school libraries varies widely throughout the United States.

School Library Media Centers: 1993-94, published by the National Center for Education Statistics in 1998, reports on the results of a school and staffing survey. It states, "Out of 164,650 school library staff, 44 percent were state-certified library media specialists, 20 percent were other non-certified professional librarians and 36 percent were other staff." (page xxi)

This survey also reported that "about half of the schools (52 percent) did not have a state-certified librarian who was there full-time," (page 6) and "20 percent of schools with library media centers did not have a librarian and 13 percent had neither a librarian nor an aide." (page 7)

JOB DESCRIPTIONS

There are four broad levels of school library staffing: Library Clerk or Paraprofessional, Library Technician, Library Media Specialist, and Library Media Coordinator.

Library Clerk or Paraprofessional
This is a classified position with general clerical background, often with a high school diploma and no specific library training required. The Library Clerk or Paraprofessional performs the daily clerical tasks in the library, including:
- circulates materials and prepares overdue notices;
- maintains circulation records and other library statistics;
- shelves materials that have been returned;
- processes new materials to be added to the collection;
- maintains the library (straightening up, creating bulletin boards, etc.);
- assists students and staff with general reference requests.

Library Technician
This is often a higher level classified position that requires some library training and experience, such as a community college library technician certificate.

The Library Technician handles the daily clerical tasks listed above, but also may be involved in more complex, technical tasks, including:
- assists in ordering materials for the library;
- catalogs and processes materials;
- oversees library automation systems and computers;
- provides instruction in the use of the library and its materials;
- trains and supervises volunteers or student aides.

Library Media Specialist
This is a certificated teaching position requiring both a teaching credential and a Library Media Specialist Certificate.

The four-part role of the Library Media Specialist is defined in *Information Power: Building Partnerships for Learning (1998)*, the national school library guidelines, as:

- teacher
- instructional partner
- information specialist
- program administrator

(pages 4-5)

The Library Media Specialist's major areas of responsibility include:
- makes collection development and purchasing decisions;
- collaborates with teachers to develop teaching units that include library and information literacy skills;
- prepares and administers the library media center budget;
- teaches students library and information literacy skills;
- supervises and trains library classified staff, volunteers and student aides;
- participates on school and district committees;
- plays a leadership role in the library planning committee.

Library Media Coordinator
Some districts have a Library Media Coordinator to coordinate the library media program throughout the school district. This position often provides training and support for clerical staff at schools where there is no credentialed library media teacher.

In addition to a Library Media Specialist Credential, the Coordinator position often requires an Administrative Credential.

WHAT YOU CAN DO

Job Description
Get a copy of your job description and read it carefully. It should give you a clear idea of the responsibilities and tasks that you are expected to handle.

Training and Support
Find out if the library staff, including library clerks, meet regularly to receive training and share information. Ask if your district has a district Library Media Coordinator who is available to provide information, support and assistance.

If there is no one available in your district, check with your county office of education or regional service center to see if there is someone who works with the staff in school libraries or if they provide classes and workshops for school library staff.

There may also be a school library organization in your area that holds regular meetings and provides a network of people willing to share information and answer your questions.

RESOURCES

American Association of School Librarians and Association for Educational Communications and Technology, *Information Power: Building Partnerships for Learning.* Chicago, IL: American Library Association, 1998.

National Center for Education Statistics, *School Library Media Centers: 1993-94.* Washington, DC: U.S. Department of Education, 1998.

LIBRARY POLICIES

Policies give long-term direction for a district and describe how this direction is to be accomplished. Policies serve both as a guide and as a protection for the library staff. The District Board of Education adopts policies for the district in many areas such as personnel, students, facilities, curriculum, and instructional materials.

> ## WHAT YOU CAN DO
> *Library staff at the school level are often not familiar with many of their district's policies. It is very important that you read and understand those policies that affect the school library and your role.*

There are generally four types of policies that have a major impact on the library:
1. **Selection policies** – give the process and criteria for selection of both textbooks/ instructional materials and for library materials.
2. **Challenge policies** – describe how complaints about materials are to be handled.
3. **Copyright policies** – explain the copyright law and fair use.
4. **Internet Acceptable Use policies** – describe procedures for student access to the Internet

This section will give you some examples of policies in these areas as well as a list of resources that can be used to get additional information about these issues.

SELECTION POLICIES

Some districts will have policies that describe how they select both instructional materials for classroom use and library materials. These policies usually contain the selection criteria and describe the process used to select textbooks and other materials which often include opportunities for parents and community members to review the materials under consideration.

Textbooks are often treated differently than library materials because textbooks are part of the normal daily curriculum and instruction in the school and are expected to be used by all students in the class. Therefore, there is usually a more stringent evaluation process with more carefully defined criteria. Textbooks in most states

must meet specific social content requirements contained in their Education Code. These often refer to the depiction of males/females, racial, ethnic and cultural groups, religion, commercial products and other specific items.

Library materials are usually not covered by these stringent requirements. Library materials generally cover a broader spectrum of topics, allowing for diverse viewpoints, various formats and levels.

Each item in the library is not required to represent all viewpoints or perspectives. One reason for this is because library materials are not required reading for all students. The materials are available for interested students and to support the various subjects in the curriculum.

Library selection policies usually refer to the principles of intellectual freedom and freedom of speech and are based on the *Library Bill of Rights* from the American Library Association (included on page 17).

Contents of a Selection Policy

1. **Philosophy/Goals and Objectives**
   This section usually refers to the Library Bill of Rights, the principles of intellectual freedom and the specific purposes, goals and objectives of the district's libraries. Statements such as, "to enrich and support the curriculum and the personal needs of the users, taking into consideration the varied interests, abilities, and maturity levels of the students served," are frequently used.

2. **Legal Responsibility**
   The Education Code and other state and federal laws and regulations may be cited. The school board has the ultimate responsibility within the district, but the policy may designate a certified library media teacher as the party responsible for the selection of library resources.

3. **Criteria for Selection**
   The criteria used to select materials may be listed in broad statements in the policy. The policy will last a long time, so it is wise not to include very specific items or topics that may have only a limited life. Statements such as, "materials will be appropriate for the subject area and for the age, emotional development, ability level, learning styles, and social development of the students for whom the materials are selected," or "materials will meet high standards of quality in factual content and presentation," are often included.

   Some policies may require that materials have been positively reviewed in certain library sources, such as *The Elementary School Library Collection* or periodicals such as the *School Library Journal, Book Report* and *Library Talk*. If that is a requirement of the policy, then it is important that there also be an alternative way to select materials that may not have been reviewed in these specific sources. Many books fit the curriculum needs of the students very well and yet will not be reviewed in these standard sources.

4. **Process for Selection**
   This section should answer the following questions:
   - Who will be involved?
   - Will there be a district or site selection committee?
   - Will the orders be reviewed and approved by someone at the district office?
   - Is there a specific timeline for selection and purchasing?

WHAT YOU CAN DO
Check to see if your district has a selection policy. If there is one, insert it into your handbook so you have it to refer to as needed. If there is no written policy, ask if there are written guidelines, understood policies, or past practices that you can follow.

CHALLENGE POLICIES

With the wide range of opinions and beliefs present in our society, it is inevitable that someone may have a complaint about a particular item in a library collection. The challenge policy will describe the process that must be followed to register this complaint and how the complaint will be addressed.

Maintaining an established process with ample opportunity to consider the opinions of those involved is designed to insure that consideration is given to the rights of the person making the complaint as well as the rights of the library's users.

Challenge policies may cover both library materials and classroom instructional materials. Parents who object to a specific instructional material may usually request that their child have an alternative. If, however, they want to restrict all students from having access to a specific item, they would need to follow the challenge policy.

Challenge policies, also called "reconsideration" or "complaint" policies, are often included as the second part of a selection policy.

Contents of a challenge policy

1. **Who can submit a complaint?**
   Some policies restrict complaints only to residents or employees of the district to keep nonresidents from making complaints about a particular book in districts other than those in which they live.

   It is important to define who may file a complaint and it is important to define who must follow the procedure. Some administrators or board members may feel that if they have a complaint, the item will be removed without going through the process. This should not happen. Everyone who wants to remove an item because of a complaint about its content should be required to follow the policy.

This doesn't mean that the library staff need to file a complaint to weed outdated or inappropriate books from the collection. That is part of their job, provided they follow criteria and have justification for why the items were weeded.

2. **How does the complaint need to be submitted?**
   Most complaints need to be in writing, identifying the specific content that is objected to and identifying the person making the complaint.

   Often a form has been developed that includes the following:
   - Name, address, phone number, and status (parent, resident, staff member) of the person making the complaint;
   - Description of the specific portions of the work which are thought to be objectionable;
   - An indication of what is being requested: removal of the material, limitations on access, restriction to certain grades or classes?

3. **Process for reconsideration**
   - Informal – after the complaint is received there may be an informal process to hear the complaint, explain the district's policies and procedures for selection.

   - Formal – if the person wishes to file a formal complaint.

   - Committee – a committee is formed, it conducts a review of the work, listens to the concerns of the person filing the complaint, and conducts any additional research needed.

- Recommendation – the committee's recommendations are sent to the Superintendent and/or the Board.

- Action – the Superintendent or the Board takes action either reaffirming the selection of the material and it stays in the library, or they may decide to take some action to change access to the material or remove it.

4. **Limits on complaints**
   How often may a person submit a complaint or how often may one item be reconsidered? Some policies do not allow additional complaints about the same item by the same person or they may not allow additional complaints about an item that has been through reconsideration until at least one year has passed.

5. **What happens to the item while it is being reconsidered?**
   Some districts pull the item from the shelf immediately until the issue is resolved, while others leave the item in the library until there is a decision by the Superintendent or Board to remove it.

> ## WHAT YOU CAN DO
> *Check your district's challenge or reconsideration procedure and be sure you are familiar with the process.*
>
> *If approached by a parent with a complaint listen carefully to their concerns and let them know what the process is. Give them a copy of the policy and the complaint form so they can decide if they want to file a formal complaint.*

COPYRIGHT POLICIES

Copyright law allows for some copying of materials by schools and libraries. However, there are limits to the copying that is protected. Library staff must be aware of the district's copyright policies and of federal copyright law as it affects the activities in their library.

> ## WHAT YOU CAN DO
> *Check your district's copyright policy and see what it requires before you make any copies of printed or media materials. Get all requests for copying in writing. Check with the Principal or a district staff person for specific procedures and directions.*

INTERNET ACCEPTABLE USE POLICIES (AUP)

Most schools are required to have a policy regarding student's access to the Internet or online sites and to provide parents with a copy of the district's written policy. District policies may require parental permission before students are allowed to access the Internet or other online resources.

> ## WHAT YOU CAN DO
> *Check your district's policy. If it requires students and parents to sign an AUP prior to accessing the Internet then you may be responsible for student use of the Internet computers in your library. Find out what the procedure is for determining whether students have a form on file. Some schools indicate this on the student ID card and require the ID card to be displayed when the student is using the Internet.*

RESOURCES

Internet:

United States Copyright Office, Library of Congress
http://www.loc.gov/copyright
   This is the main site for the copyright office. From here you can download information circulars, such as Circular 21, "Reproduction of Copyrighted Works by Educators and Librarians," which contains basic information on some of the most important legislative provisions and other documents dealing with reproduction by librarians and educators.

Books:

Brunwelheide, Janis H., *The Copyright Primer for Librarians and Educators, 2nd edition.* Chicago, IL: American Library Association and National Education Association, 1995.

Fresno County Office of Education, *School Library Standards.* Fresno, CA: Fresno County Office of Education, 1998.

Simpson, Carol Mann, *Copyright for Schools: A Practical Guide, 3rd edition.* Worthington, OH: Linworth Publishing, Inc., 2001.

The following selection policy and *Request for Reconsideration of Library Resources* is reprinted with permission from *School Library Standards* published by the Fresno County Office of Education, 1998.

SAMPLE POLICY:
Selection of Library Materials

Purpose: To ensure that students and teachers are provided access to a wide variety of appropriate print and nonprint resources.

I. Statement of Policy

The policy of the district/school is to provide a wide range of library materials on all levels of difficulty, with diversity of appeal, and the presentation of different points of view and to allow the review of allegedly inappropriate resources through established procedures.

II. Goals for Selection

In the selection of library materials, the district/school adheres to the principles of the American Library Association's *Library Bill of Rights.* In order to assure that the library media center is an integral part of the educational program of the school, the following selection objectives are applied:

- To provide materials that will enrich and support the curricula and personal needs of the users, taking into consideration their varied interests, abilities and learning styles.
- To provide a background of information which will enable pupils to make intelligent judgment in their daily lives.
- To provide materials with varying points of view on current and historical issues so that users may develop the skills of critical analysis.
- To place materials which realistically represent our pluralistic society and reflect the contributions made by these groups and individuals to our American heritage.
- To place principle above personal opinion and reason above prejudice in the selection of materials of the highest quality in order to assure a comprehensive library media collection appropriate for the users.

III. Legal Responsibility and Delegation

Ultimate responsibility for the selection of library resources rests with the school board. The superintendent, principals, directors, resource teachers, teachers, library media teachers, and other staff members operate within the framework of policies determined by the board. The responsibility for coordinating and recommending the selection and purchase of resources is delegated to the certificated library media teachers or if none is available, the director of curriculum development or principal.

IV. Criteria for Selection

A. Educational goals of the school/ district, individual student learning modes, teaching styles, curricula needs, faculty and student needs, existing materials, and networking arrangements should be considered in developing the ¡library media collection.

B. Library resources shall:
- Support and be consistent with the general educational goals of the school/district and the aims and objectives of the individual school.
- Meet high standards of quality in factual content and presentation.

© 2001 Santa Clara County Office of Education

- Be appropriate for the subject area and for the age, emotional development, ability level, learning styles, and social development of the students for whom the materials are selected.
- Have aesthetic, literary and social values.
- In physical format and appearance, be suitable for their intended use.
- Be developed by competent authors and producers.
- Be designed to help students gain an awareness of our pluralistic society as well as an understanding of the many important contributions made to our civilization by women and minority and ethnic groups.
- Motivate students and staff to examine their own attitude and to comprehend their own duties, responsibilities, rights, and privileges as participating citizens in our society.
- Be selected for their strengths rather than rejected for their weaknesses.

V. Procedure for Selection

A. The certified library media teacher or if none is available, the director of curriculum development or principal, shall use recognized selection tools and processes in selecting library resources.

B. Recommendations for purchase shall be solicited from teachers and students.

C. Gift and sponsored materials shall be judged by the criteria in Section IV and shall be accepted or rejected by these criteria.

D. Selection is an ongoing process which shall include the removal of resources no longer appropriate and the replacement of lost and worn resources that may still may be of education value.

E. All non-book materials (television, video, software, etc.) shall be selected on the following basis:
   1. the materials shall meet legal compliance;
   2. appropriate documentation shall be on file with the site library media personnel;
   3. be consistent with recommendations from the California Clearinghouse for instructional materials.

VI. Guidelines for Age Appropriate Usage

It is the responsibility of the principal to assure students will have access to age appropriate materials. Practices will be in place at each site to guide students and their instructors in the selection of age/grade appropriate resources.

VII. Reconsideration of Library Resources

A. Statement of Policy

Any resident or employee of the district may formally challenge library resources used in the district's educational program on the basis of appropriateness. This procedure is for the purpose of considering the opinions of those persons in the schools and the community who are not directly involved in the selection process.

B. Request for Informal Reconsideration
   1. The school receiving a complaint regarding a library resource shall try to resolve the issue informally.
      a. The principal or library personnel shall explain to the questioner the school's selection procedure, criteria, and qualifications of those persons selecting the resource.

b. The principal or other appropriate staff shall explain to the questioner the place the resource occupies in the education program, its intended educational usefulness, and additional information regarding its use, or refer the party to someone who can identify and explain the use of resource.

c. If the questioner wishes to file a formal challenge, a copy of the district *Request for Reconsideration of Library Resources Form* shall be provided by the principal to the party concerned.

C. Request for Formal Reconsideration

1. If resolution is not obtained through the informal reconsideration procedure, the questioner may request a district *Request for Reconsideration of Library Resources* from the site principal.

2. The *Request for Reconsideration of Library Resources Form* shall be completed and signed by the questioner and filed with the principal.

3. The superintendent shall be informed of the formal complaint.

4. Within five business days of the filing of the form the principal shall submit a copy of the complaint to the Reconsideration Committee.

5. The Reconsideration Committee shall be made up of:
   a. one member of the district staff chosen by the superintendent;
   b. one member of the school teaching staff chosen by the school staff;
   c. a library media teacher/library media specialist chosen by the superintendent;
   d. one parent member of the School Site Council;
   e. other appointee as directed by the superintendent, principal, or library media director.

6. Access to challenged materials shall **not** be restricted during the reconsideration process.

7. The committee chair shall distribute copies of challenged material to the members.

8. After the committee has reviewed the challenged material a conference is then arranged with the reconsideration committee and the:
   a. site principal,
   b. site library media teacher and/or other appropriate staff, and
   c. challenger.

9. The sole criteria for the final decision is the appropriateness of the material for its intended educational use.

   The Reconsideration Committee's final decision will be to:
   a. take no removal action;
   b. remove the challenged material from the total school environment;
   c. allow students to use alternate titles, approved by school personnel involved;
   d. limit the educational use of the challenged material.

10. The decision of the Reconsideration Committee is binding for the district. If the challenger is not satisfied with the decision, a request may be made to place the matter on the agenda of

the next regularly scheduled meeting of the board.

11. Requests to reconsider materials which have previously been before the Reconsideration Committee must receive approval of a majority of the committee members before the materials will again be reconsidered. Every *Request for Reconsideration of Library Resources Form* shall be acted upon by the Reconsideration Committee.

SAMPLE REQUEST FOR RECONSIDERATION
OF LIBRARY RESOURCES

Initiated by:_____

Telephone Number:_____   Address:_____

Name of School: _____

Representing:

   Self:_____   Group (give name of group):_____

   Organization (give name of organization):_____

Resource Challenged:
  Book:

      Author:_____

      Title: _____

      Publisher:_____

      Copyright Date: _____   Hardcover or paperback: _____

  Non-Book:

      Type of Resource: _____
                (Magazine, video, filmstrip, record, person, community resource, etc.)

      Title/Name: _____

      Publisher/Producer:_____

Please respond to the following questions. Feel free to use additional sheets of paper.
1. Did you review the entire item? If not, what section did you review?
2. To what did you object? Please be specific.
3. What do you believe is the main idea of this material?
4. What do you feel might be the result of a student using this material?
5. Is there anything good about this material?
6. Are you aware of the judgment of this material by professional critics?
7. In your opinion, for what age group would this material be more appropriate?
8. In place of this material, would you care to recommend other material that you consider more appropriate?

_____   _____
Signature   Date

Library Bill of Rights

The American Library Association affirms that all libraries are forums for information and ideas, and that the following basic policies should guide their services.

I. Books and other library resources should be provided for the interest, information, and enlightenment of all people of the community the library serves. Materials should not be excluded because of the origin, background, or views of those contributing to their creation.

II. Libraries should provide materials and information presenting all points of view on current and historical issues. Materials should not be proscribed or removed because of partisan or doctrinal disapproval.

III. Libraries should challenge censorship in the fulfillment of their responsibility to provide information and enlightenment.

IV. Libraries should cooperate with all persons and groups concerned with resisting abridgment of free expression \and free access to ideas.

V. A person's right to use a library should not be denied or abridged because of origin, age, background, or views.

VI. Libraries which make exhibit spaces and meeting rooms available to the public they serve should make such facilities available on an equitable basis, regardless of the beliefs or affiliations of individuals or groups requesting their use.

Adopted June 18, 1948. Amended February 2, 1961, and January 23, 1980, inclusion of "age" reaffirmed January 23, 1996, by the ALA Council.

Access to Resources and Services in the School Library Media Program: An Interpretation of the Library Bill of Rights

The school library media program plays a unique role in promoting intellectual freedom. It serves as a point of voluntary access to information and ideas and as a learning laboratory for students as they acquire critical thinking and problem solving skills needed in a pluralistic society. Although the educational level and program of the school necessarily shape the resources and services of a school library media program, the principles of the Library Bill of Rights apply equally to all libraries, including school library media programs.

School library media professionals assume a leadership role in promoting the principles of intellectual freedom within the school by providing resources and services that create and sustain an atmosphere of free inquiry. School library media professionals work closely with teachers to integrate instructional activities in classroom units designed to equip students to locate, evaluate, and use a broad range of ideas effectively. Through resources, programming, and educational processes, students and teachers experience the free and robust debate characteristic of a democratic society.

School library media professionals cooperate with other individuals in building collections of resources appropriate to the developmental and maturity levels of students. These collections provide resources which support the curriculum and are consistent with the philosophy, goals, and objectives of the school district. Resources in school library media collections represent diverse points of view on current as well as historical issues.

While English is, by history and tradition, the customary language of the United States, the languages in use in any given community may vary. Schools serving communities in which other languages are used make efforts to accommodate the needs of students for whom English is a second language. To support these efforts, and to ensure equal access to resources and services, the school library media program provides resources which reflect the linguistic pluralism of the community.

Members of the school community involved in the collection development process employ educational criteria to select resources unfettered by their personal, political, social, or religious views. Students and educators served by the school library media program have access to resources and services free of constraints resulting from personal, partisan, or doctrinal disapproval. School library media professionals resist efforts by individuals to define what is appropriate for all students or teachers to read, view, or hear, or access via electronic means.

Major barriers between students and resources includebut are not limirted to: imposing age or grade level restrictions on the use of resources, limiting the use of interlibrary loan and access to electronic information, charging fees for information in specific formats, requiring permission from parents or teachers, establishing restricted shelves or closed collections, and labeling. Policies, procedures, and rules related to the use of resources and services support free and open access to information.

The school board adopts policies that guarantee students access to a broad range of ideas. These include policies on collection development and procedures for the review of resources about which concerns have been raised. Such policies, developed by the persons in the school community, provide for a timely and fair hearing and assure that procedures are applied equitably to all expressions of concern. School library media professionals implement district policies and procedures in the school.

Adopted July 2, 1986; amended January 10, 1990; July 12, 2000, by the ALA Council.

SAMPLE POLICY:
Copyright

COPYRIGHTED MATERIALS
BOARD POLICY

It is the policy of the Board that the District shall inform employees of the provisions of all copyright laws and monitor adherence to these laws. The Board recognizes that the Copyright Revision Act, Public Law 94-553 and 96-517, makes it illegal to duplicate copyrighted materials without authorization. The Board further recognizes that severe penalties are provided for unauthorized copying of any materials (printed, audio, visual, and computer programs).

Criteria used to determine authorized copying, as well as prohibitions against unauthorized copying, may not be universally understood by employees of the District. For this reason, the Superintendent shall develop guidelines which clarify the duplication of copyrighted materials.

The following acceptable use policy and *Acceptable Use Contract* are reprinted with permission from the Santa Clara County Office of Education, 1998.

SAMPLE POLICY:
Acceptable Use

STUDENT USE OF TECHNOLOGY
BOARD POLICY
It is the policy of the Board that appropriate technological tools and training to allow students to function successfully in society shall be available to students enrolled in County Office of Education programs. Technology will be used to support alternative and diverse educational delivery systems. The Superintendent or designee shall develop and maintain a plan to ensure that appropriate and current technology is available and integrated into the classroom.

The Superintendent or designee shall also establish regulations prohibiting students enrolled in County Office of Education programs to use the technological tools provided by the Office to access harmful matter on the Internet/school networks, pursuant to Education Code §51870.5.

Santa Clara County Office of Education
Internet and School Network Systems Acceptable Use Contract

❑ **I will use the Internet and school network systems only for educational purposes.** I will not use the school's systems for commercial, political, or personal purposes.

❑ **I will be considerate.** I will not send messages which are abusive or threatening or contain offensive language; destroy data through uploading or creating computer viruses; or read, copy, or modify other users' mail.

❑ **I will only use the files, accounts, or passwords that are assigned to me.** I will respect the privacy and confidentiality of others.

❑ **I will be careful.** I will not reveal my home address or personal phone number or the addresses and phone numbers of others on the Internet or school network systems.

❑ **I will not hold the SCCOE responsible for damages or inaccuracies on the systems.** I understand the following: that the SCCOE makes no warranties for the services it is providing; that the SCCOE will not be responsible for any damages suffered while on the systems; and that the SCCOE does not have responsibility for the accuracy of information obtained through its services.

❑ **I will not access harmful matter and misuse the systems.** I understand that "harmful matter" means that which shows or describes sexual conduct in an offensive way and which has no literary, artistic, political, or scientific value for minors. I understand that "misuse the systems" means sending or receiving data which is discriminatory or which promotes illegal or unethical activities.

❑ **I may lose access to the systems if I do not follow the rules.** I understand that the use of the systems is a privilege, not a right. Inappropriate use may result in cancellation of this privilege.

Instructions to Students and Parents or Guardians: Please sign and return this contract to your school. Signatures from the student and parent or guardian are required so that the student may access the school's systems.

Student Signature

I understand that any violations of the above provisions may result in disciplinary or legal action. I agree to report any access to harmful matter and misuse of the systems to the principal or designee.

Student Signature _____ Date _____

Parent or Guardian Signature

As the parent or guardian, I understand that it is impossible for the SCCOE to restrict access to all controversial material, and I will not hold the SCCOE responsible for materials acquired on the systems. I agree to report any access to harmful matter and misuse of the systems to the principal or designee.

Parent or Guardian Signature _____ Date _____

LIBRARY HANDBOOK

A library handbook is useful for communicating with students, parents and faculty and can be a valuable public relations tool. Libraries are mysterious places to people who are not familiar with their collections, organization and rules. Having a Handbook can help to demystify the library and clearly explain what the library is and what is expected of those who use it.

Library Handbook

Whether it is a booklet, a pamphlet, or available on the school's web page, the handbook must be clear, attractive, and concise.

Suggested handbook contents:
- Mission and goals of the library;
- Rules for student behavior;
- Discipline and consequences for violation of rules;
- Check out, overdue and fine policies;
- Staff list;
- Hours open;
- Selection and challenge policies;
- Services and collections available;
- Special programs and activities.

Rules

The rules for the library must coordinate with the school's rules and discipline policy.

It is recommended that the library not be used as a form of punishment. Also, don't make rules you do not intend to enforce.

In addition to the normal school rules for behavior, the school library rules might include:
- Be considerate of others.
- Don't make loud noises.

- Put materials away after using them.
- No food or drink allowed in the library.
- Share resources – computers, reference tools.
- You must have your ID to check out materials.
- Students must be engaged in constructive work (homework, browsing, reading).

Here are examples of rules from other librarians that were posted to LM_NET (see the Resources list for more information on LM_NET.)

- My posted rules:
    - Be prepared.
    - Respect your environment.
    - Be responsible.
    - Obey all school rules.
    - Respect others.

- Our library rules are simple:
  Respect People/Respect Property

- Doug Johnson mentions these rules in his book, *The Indispensable Librarian (1997):*
    1. Be doing something productive.
    2. Be doing it in a way that allows others to be productive.
    3. Be respectful of other persons and property.

Communicate the rules

Rules can be communicated in many ways:
- create a large poster with the rules for all to see;
- put the rules on a bookmark;
- include the rules in your library handbook;
- include the rules on your web page.

Teach the rules

Librarians have tried many ways to teach and reinforce the rules for appropriate behavior in the library. Here are ideas, some of which came from LM_NET:

- Have some students model correct and incorrect behavior. Students enjoy the "acting" and everyone gets a clear view of exactly what is expected and what is unacceptable.

- Make a cube from foam board using six 6-inch squares. Put a sad face on three squares, the others have happy faces. Sit in a circle with the students and give each child a turn rolling the cube. If it lands with a happy face showing up, ask the student to say something that is GOOD to do in the library. If they roll a sad face they say something that is a BAD thing to do.

  Print out each rule in very large type and post them on the wall next to where you sit, in case someone needs help remembering.

- Put the library rules on a bookmark with a graphic related to the rules that can be colored on the back. If the student returns the bookmark colored in each week, they may check out an extra book.

- Collect props and put them in a box. Pull one out at a time. Then tell the students how that item relates to how they should behave in the library and take care of books. Some examples:
  - an empty food container (don't eat or drink in the library);
  - a toy dog (don't let your pets get your books);
  - a noisemaker (don't make loud sounds in the library);
  - a calendar (remember to return your books on time);
  - glasses (to remind them to look at the person who is talking);
  - crayons and markers (never to be used in a library book);
  - a band-aid (please bring your books to school to get fixed).

- Put objects that relate to the library rules (see suggestions above) around the library. As the students watch you move around the library explaining how it is organized and where things are located, you can find each object and it will remind you (and your students) about the rule.

RESOURCES:

Internet:
LM_NET on the World Wide Web
http://askeric.org/lm_net/
This is the home page for LM_NET, the school library media listserv. Here you can learn more about LM_NET and how to sign up. If you don't wish to receive all of the messages, you can search the archives for specific topics and see the messages that were posted in the past.

Books:
Johnson, Doug, *The Indispensable Librarian: Surviving (and Thriving) in School Media Centers in the Information Age.* Worthington, OH: Linworth Publishing Inc., 1997.

LIBRARY ORGANIZATION

You may believe that there isn't much you can do about the organization of your library. After all, the shelves are set in place and the walls, windows and doors aren't going to move. Though this is true, there are a number of things that you can do to change the organization of your library without major renovation:

- most furniture can be rearranged;
- some shelving can be moved;
- collections can be placed on different shelves;
- traffic patterns can be changed, and;
- the room environment can be enhanced.

EXAMPLE

Alice Bethke once worked in a school library shaped like a long narrow "v." It had 11 doors that could be used as entrances and exits and was often used only as a hallway. The circulation desk was in the center of the "v" with tables and collections scattered throughout. Though she couldn't change the location of the bookshelves, she was able to do a lot.

Her solution was to pull the tables into one large teaching area located right in the center of the "v." The on-line catalog and the counter height reference shelves also were relocated close to the center near the circulation desk. Furniture and other counter height shelves served as a divider or traffic stop, making it more difficult for students to use the library as a hall.

She then decorated the center area extensively, using a different theme each year, with posters, mobiles, and a piñata hanging from the ceiling. This made the center so attractive and inviting that students were drawn there making them easy to see and supervise.

You <u>do</u> have the power to change your environment in many ways.

Whenever you organize your library, keep in mind these rules:

GOLDEN RULES OF LIBRARY ORGANIZATION

- *Create An Inviting Environment*
- *Consider Students' Learning First*
- *Make It As Flexible As Possible*
- *Be Sure All Areas Can Be Supervised Easily*
- *Consider The Flow Of Traffic*

by Alice Bethke
Santa Clara Unified School District

How do these golden rules apply to library organization?

Create an Inviting Environment

The library should be a warm, welcoming place for students and teachers. The use of light, color, displays and signage contribute a great deal to the environment of the library. The goal is for students to want to be in and to use the library. More information on displays is provided in a later chapter.

Consider Students' Learning First

Bookstores are arranged in a certain way to make it easier for customers to find what they want in order to increase sales. Public libraries are also in the business of providing materials to their customers as easily as possible. However, school libraries are in the business of teaching students "to be effective users of ideas and information."

When arranging your library keep in mind that students need to learn the skills of information literacy. They need to know how to look things up and find them on the shelf and how to carry these skills with them to other settings.

School libraries keep most nonfiction materials on the shelves in Dewey order and fiction alphabetically by author. School libraries have their materials in a logical sequence on the shelves so students can make sense of the arrangement. See the section titled, "Variations on the Theme" for pros and cons of different arrangements.

Make It As Flexible As Possible

The library holds many different activities. An elementary library can have primary level children sitting on the floor listening to a book being read, an upper grade class working in teams to develop a research report and the School Site Council meeting in the library after school.

A high school library may have several classes working on different projects at the same time, while individual students are doing research. When organizing a library, think of many possible uses and make your design as flexible as you can.

Be Sure All Areas Can Be Supervised Easily

In order to supervise students effectively a staff member standing at the circulation desk should be able to see all areas of the library. When planning for tall shelves or placement of furniture think about the "hidden" places that may be out of your line of sight where students can either get into mischief or cannot be seen if they need assistance.

The on-line catalog, computer reference stations and reference shelves are all places where students need the most assistance. These should be placed close to the circulation desk and in clear view. Computers should be placed so the monitor screens are easily seen to supervise student use.

Consider The Flow Of Traffic

How will students enter and exit the library? Where will books be returned and checked out? These functions usually cause congestion, so plan for them. Do you have sufficient space for people to walk around tables and computer stations, especially if they are being used. Avoid dead ends in your aisles, if possible, as this causes congestion.

How are the materials arranged on the shelves? Do they flow in a logical order so students can find materials easily or do students need to criss-cross the library to find what they need?

PLANNING CONSIDERATIONS

Some things to think about when planning for library space:

- Electrical outlets – where are they located? If electricity is at a premium, you won't want to put shelves in front of the few outlets you have.

- Network connections – in addition to electricity, most of your computer stations will require a network connection. This is often overlooked in library planning, even by the professionals.

- Windows – keep windows clear to maximize natural light to the library.

- Doors – you can design the flow of traffic by designating certain doors for entrance and exit, but you cannot block doors that provide emergency exits.

- Aisles – be sure to have at least 42 inch wide aisles for access by everyone, including the disabled.

- Shelving height – shelving of picture/easy books should be 42 inches or less, elementary and middle school shelving 60 inches or less, while high school shelving may be taller.

- Shelving needs – Allow one linear foot of shelving for:
    - 20 picture/easy books
    - 12 elementary fiction/ nonfiction books
    - 10 high school fiction/nonfiction books
    - 8 reference books

RESOURCES

Books:

Baule, Steven M., *Facilities Planning for School and Library Media Technology Centers.* Worthington, OH: Linworth Publishing Co., 1999.

Erikson, Rolf and Carolyn Markuson, *Designing a School Library Media Center for the Future.* Chicago, IL: American Library Association, 2001.

Hart, Thomas L., *Creative Ideas for Library Media Center Facilities.* Englewood, CO: Libraries Unlimited, 1990.

VARIATIONS ON THE THEME

There are many variations on the standard organization of a school library. Each of those variations has pro's and con's. Here are some of the variations you might encounter in an elementary school.

COLLECTION AREA	ALTERNATE ORGANIZATION	ISSUES AND CONCERNS	NOTES
E Books – Separate section for: • Beginning readers. • Caldecott or other award-winning books. • Predictable books, ABC books, circle stories, etc.	• Teachers may ask for separate sections in the library.	• The more divisions that are created in a library, the more a student must learn to be successful. • Some of the divisions teachers request are temporary in nature.	• Stickers can be put on the spine to designate beginning readers, award books, etc. • Special display of books can be set aside for teachers working on a unit.
Fiction Books: • Separate sections for types of books (such as historical fiction or mystery stories). • Separate sections for series of books.	• Teachers and students may request separate sections for these types of books.	• Multiple places to look for books makes the library more difficult to use for patrons. • Other libraries do not use the same divisions so students are not acquiring lifelong skills.	• Vendors have stickers for awards and types of fiction. • Special displays can be created as needed. • Student can be taught how to find materials by using library tools such as the catalog.
Biographies	• Standard cataloging in public and academic libraries now places biographies under the profession of the subject .	• Teachers often teach biography units and require students to read a biography. • It is difficult to lead students to biographies if they are separated into different Dewey areas. • Students may know a person they want to read about, but not know their profession. • Subject headings for biographies are under the name of the biographee (last name, first name). • People have multiple professions.	• Most school libraries and children's libraries keep biographies in a separate section (usually designated "92" or "B"). This means that a school profile must be given to the vendor for books ordered preprocessed.
Reading Incentive Programs, such as Accelerated Reader, Reading Counts, and so forth.	• Libraries are requested to shelve or identify these books by level. It is better to integrate these books together with other books on the shelves.	• Students may tend to ignore other books that aren't identified as part of the program and may miss good titles if they are shelved separately. • The more separate places that students have to look for materials, the more difficult it is for them, and they don't learn how to use the library. • When programs change, the book markings, shelving, and so forth, would need to change.	• Printed lists of materials in these programs can be provided. • MARC records have a reading level tag that can be used.
Non-Print Materials Section	• Easier to shelve if nonprint is kept separate.	• Materials on same subject are in different places if shelved by type of material. • Nonprint should be shelved according to Dewey Decimal Classification.	• Consider who is permitted to check out the materials. Integrate if students can check out and separate if they are for teachers only.

TOUR OF LIBRARY

Use this form to take a tour of your library and make notes on your observations. Sometimes it's difficult to see things in our own environment. Ask a trusted co-worker to visit your library and jot down their observations to help you improve your library's environment.

Did you feel welcome?

Would students feel welcome?

Comments/rating on:

Rating: 1=poor, 3=fair, 5=excellent

Layout:	1	2	3	4	5
shelving	1	2	3	4	5
circulation area	1	2	3	4	5
supervision of students	1	2	3	4	5
Traffic patterns:	1	2	3	4	5
Furniture:	1	2	3	4	5
arrangement	1	2	3	4	5
comfort	1	2	3	4	5
availability	1	2	3	4	5
Lighting:	1	2	3	4	5
Displays:	1	2	3	4	5
centers	1	2	3	4	5
themes	1	2	3	4	5
ties to classroom work	1	2	3	4	5
Directional signs:	1	2	3	4	5

Suggestions for improvement:

Summarize the library using 5-6 descriptive terms:

SAFETY

The list below presents some ideas on issues of safety that might be present in school libraries.

WHAT YOU CAN DO

Check your school safety plan for specific information or ask about safety training that might be offered in your district.

SHELVES
- Secure/brace shelves to prevent them from falling in case of earthquake.

- Do not overload the top shelf or place heavy items on the top of shelves.

ELECTRICAL
- Do not overload electrical circuits by plugging in too many cords.

- Use three wire grounded plugs when needed.

- Check plugs and cords regularly for wear.

- Be very careful about the placement of cords.

- Batteries should be stored in a cool, dark place.

FACILITY
- Examine carpets, furniture and other areas for wear, holes, splinters, sharp edges and request repairs when needed.

- Keep exits clear and well marked.

EQUIPMENT
- Keep information booklets for all equipment – these contain safety tips.

- Copy equipment operating instructions, laminate and keep with equipment.

- Be aware of specific handling requirements for equipment.

- Carts – use only approved, safe carts which will not easily tip over.

- Secure large equipment, such as television monitors, to carts.

- Laminators, laser printers, copy machines and other equipment get very hot and need to be handled with extreme care.

- Be sure equipment that needs ventilation is in an open area and additional ventilation is available, if needed.

27

The library should be a warm, exciting, welcoming place where students want to be. This can be achieved through a number of ways:
- use of the space;
- flow and arrangement of the furniture;
- signs and directional information;
- way materials are displayed or merchandised (think of your local bookstore);
- displays and bulletin boards.

The library can be more inviting through the use of flowers, plants, an aquarium, mobiles, wall hangings. This section will give you ideas that you can use to improve the environment of your library.

DISPLAYS

There are many opportunities for displays of various types in your library. Schedule them throughout the year so students and staff will have new reasons to come into the library. In addition to items in display cases, there are many other types of displays: bulletin boards, table or shelf top displays, wall or ceiling hangings, floor displays and merchandising displays.

Displays can serve many purposes:
- Instructional – teach concepts, facts, or reinforce skills;
- Informational – make students aware of rules, new books;
- Motivational – encourage students to read;
- Library management – manage class visits, checkouts, other daily activities;
- Decorative – enhance the environment in the library.

Displays may serve several purposes at once. A reading motivation display may also teach and be decorative. Thinking through your display in advance will help you get the most from your efforts.

WHAT YOU CAN DO

There are several steps in planning and creating displays. Give some advance thought to your plans so you will be more effective and save considerable time.

Planning Your Display

1. Audience – who is the target audience for this display – students of all ages, primary grade students, boys, teachers?
2. Purpose – what do you want to have happen as a result of this display?
3. Theme – what is the content and the slogan or title of the display?
4. Materials – what do you want to include, what materials are needed to create the display?
5. Sketch ideas for the display - How will it look? Where will you locate items? This doesn't need to be an elaborate illustration, but can serve as a guide to help you as you create and assemble materials.
6. Create or gather materials needed.

7. Mockup – arrange the materials on a table or the floor so you can see how everything will look and how it will fit in the space you have.
8. Put it all together – step back and admire your work.
9. Photograph it for future reference – if the photograph is scanned, or if you use a digital camera, the photo can easily be included in your school newsletter or web page as a public relations item.

DISPLAY CONSIDERATIONS

- Use a background or backdrop to unify a display – fabric is easy to work with.

- Vary the height of items – use boxes or other items to give height to the display.

- If displaying photos or flat artwork, mat the item to make it stand out.

- Provide captions so visitors know what is displayed and why it is important.

- Include props, real stuff, that relates to the display. For example, a display of student paintings and sculpture about sports might include a stopwatch, a pair of running shoes, or a bat and glove.

TYPES OF DISPLAYS

- Student work – drawings, sculptures, models, wood work, posters, especially if the work was researched in, or relates to, the library.

- Special displays – from students and staff such as hobbies, family history, crafts. If displaying anything of value be sure it is secure. A locked display case is perfect. (If you don't have one, perhaps a staff member or parent who does woodworking would create one for the library.)

- Hanging displays – kites, models, student-made piñatas, stars and planets. Some vendors sell hooks, magnetic holders and other supplies to hang materials from the ceiling.

GETTING IDEAS

You can get ideas from many places; just keep your eyes open. Notice how things are displayed, how they are grouped, the materials that are used, any catchy phrases on signs or themes used by others.

WHAT YOU CAN DO

Carry around a small notebook or stack of index cards and jot down or sketch ideas as they come to you or cut out pages and illustrations. These can be filed for future use.

Real objects can be used effectively in displays. This wheelbarrow and packets of seeds set the stage for books on plants and gardening.

30

Good sources for ideas are:
- Magazines
- Catalogs and brochures
- In-store and window displays
- Other libraries
- Greeting cards
- Food packaging
- Billboards

MATERIALS

Almost anything can be a useful resource for bulletin boards and displays. Bulletin boards are much more interesting when many different kinds of materials are used. Save and store a lot of different things that look interesting.

Some ideas for materials to save are:
- String, rope
- Leaves, pressed flowers, dried flowers, branches
- Fabric, lace, trim, yarn
- Artificial vines, silk flowers
- Beads, jewelry
- Clothes, denim jeans pockets, scarves, hats, shoes
- Containers, boxes, paper bags
- Popsicle sticks, plastic ware, paper plates
- Wood, picket fence, chicken wire
- Balloons
- Candy, empty food packages
- Book pockets, envelopes
- Toys
- Stuffed animals

Sources for materials include:
- Decorating/fabric stores for samples of wallpaper and remnants of fabric and trim.

- Printing companies and newspapers may have remnants of paper.

- Yard sales and flea markets for props, decorations, costumes.

- Second hand stores.

- Stores may have containers, old display props, packing materials.

- Parents may have access to materials through their work or hobbies.

- Field trips – locations visited may have materials.

MERCHANDISING

Think of how your local bookstore displays their books – face out. Look at a book - the most attractive part is the cover and, yet, on your shelves the covers cannot be seen. The only part that shows is the narrow spine.

New books are displayed on a table, standing up. Notice the easy to read sign and the bright flowers used to make the display attractive.

Find ways to show off your books by their covers:
- Stand individual books on the empty end of each shelf.

- Display books on flat surfaces – the center of your tables, shelf tops, on top of the card catalog or the window sill.
- Purchase stands to display the books or you can use plate holders.
- Create spaces to display books using plastic crates, boxes, unused furniture.
- Use plastic gutters along walls or shelf ends to display books (See an article with photos at Jim Trelease's web site - http://www.trelease-on-reading.com/whats_nu_raingutters.html).

BULLETIN BOARDS

Bulletin boards are the easiest display to create because most classrooms and school libraries include a bulletin board or a wall surface that can be used as a bulletin board. There are many books of ideas for bulletin boards, but with a little imagination and some creativity you can create your very own masterpieces.

SPACE FOR BULLETIN BOARDS

Many people think that the only space that can be used for displays is a place on the wall with a tackable surface that's called a "bulletin board." However, there are many other spaces that can serve the same purpose as a bulletin board.

Other spaces to consider:
- Create a new space for a bulletin board by covering a large cardboard box.

- Tape laminated items to the floor to make a trail all over the library.

- Put a display board on an easel, on the blackboard chalk rail, or propped on the furniture.

- Use the front of your desk, the side of the file cabinet or other furniture.

- Use that small wall space next to the door for a long, narrow bulletin board.

- A window can be a bulletin board – laminate separate items and hang the laminate in the window so the sun can shine between the items, or create transparencies of student work to hang in the window.

- Hang bulletin board displays from the ceiling – foam board is both lightweight and sturdy, or create a fabric banner.

- Use the wall up high, above the stacks, for large displays that can be easily seen from student height.

- Hang a small bulletin board on a door.

- Secure a large branch in a bucket or anchored in wood and hang items to make a 3-D bulletin board.

BACKGROUNDS

The background sets the stage for the bulletin board or display. It unifies the collection and helps to tie it together.

Ideas for background materials:
- fadeless bulletin board paper
- painted burlap or print fabric (seasonal prints)
- wallpaper

- wrapping paper
- cellophane
- bubble wrap
- brown wrapping paper
- felt
- hook and loop fabric
- wood
- shelf paper
- newspapers
- sheets, tablecloths, shower curtains.

Remember, that the background shouldn't be so "busy" that it distracts from the display.

Creating a new bulletin board from scratch takes a lot of work, yet, in order to maintain student interest and freshen the look of the library, the board needs to be changed several times throughout the school year.

Saving time on the background or finding ways to recycle the background will make it easier to change the board design regularly. Fadeless bulletin board paper will last a long time without leaving tell tale fading from previous materials.

Other ideas for saving time on backgrounds include:

- Layers – background paper can be put on a bulletin board in layers. As new boards go up during the year, remove a layer at a time to reveal the new colored background.

- Graphic – create a year of themes around one major symbol. A tree, for example, can stay on the board all year, but can hold different objects, such as fall leaves, apple cut outs, spring flowers, icicles, birds, and butterflies.

- One background – keep the same background, but vary the border according to the theme or the season to make the board look new.

- Fabric background – can last a long time and does not show the marks from pins, thumb tacks or staples. It can also be washed and reused.

- Basic structure – Keep the background and structure the same, just vary the captions. A quiz board could have flaps with questions, students lift the flap to see the answer. A board with pockets that hold cards listing books available in the library could have different categories on the pockets each month.

BORDERS

Borders define the edge of the bulletin board and help to unify the display. Borders can also reinforce the theme of the bulletin board. They can be created out of items found or created by students.

Border ideas:
- Hands – trace and cut around student hand shapes.
- Leaves – fall leaves or leaf shapes cut from paper.
- Socks, gloves, hats, or other clothing.
- Rope, fringe, giant rick-rack.

Borders of paper or tag board can be laminated in sections and attached to the bulletin board with double stick tape. This makes it easy to remove, store, and reuse them over again.

BEYOND THE FRAME

You are not limited to the traditional bulletin board frame. Many billboards you see by the highway extend their image beyond the edges of the billboard to be different and to attract interest – you can do the same. Try these ideas to go beyond the frame:

- Hot air balloon – extend above the board using yarn to connect the board to a large hot air balloon that floats up to the ceiling.

The balloon starts on the bulletin board and soars to the ceiling. The tree is made from twisted brown paper bags to simulate bark. It starts in the corner and extends along both walls.

- Animal – put an elephant head, trunk, tail and feet around the board.

- Wrap around – create giant hands (use gloves stuffed with newspaper) to hold the board and put a head with only hair, eyes and a nose that pokes down over the top of the board.

- Graphics can extend beyond the edge (a plant could grow above the board).

- Link to a display – graphics on a bulletin board can be linked to items on a table or display set in front using yarn.

- Truck or train – extend the border to create the wheels and cab of a truck or the wheels and front of a train locomotive. If you have several bulletin boards in a row, make a complete train with locomotive and caboose.

LETTERING

Letters need to be clear and large enough to be easily read from a distance. Letters are usually cut out of paper and laminated, but you can be creative with lettering to make your bulletin board or display unique.

Many different materials and ideas can be used for lettering, you are not limited to die cut or printed letters. Die cut letters are cut using a "die," usually a block of wood with a metal shape embedded in it and a foam backing. These are used in a press to cut out the letters. Two companies that sell these die cut machines are Ellison® and AccuCut®.

Here are just a few other lettering ideas for you to consider:

- Mount letters on shapes, such as leaves, hearts, balloons.

- Cut letters with fancy scissors that give a shaped edge.

- Die cut letters from contact paper – they will be self-sticking and easy to attach to the background.

- Enlarge computer generated letters and copy or print onto different paper.

- Write in script or print out words from your computer, then cut out around the total word, following the shapes of the letters, leaving a border around the word.

- Die cut letters from newspaper, wallpaper or wrapping paper (remember, if you have a one-way design, cut papers in the same direction).

- Hand tear paper into letter shapes.

- Use chalk on dark colored paper.

- Cut out words or letters from magazines or catalogs.

- Use die cut shapes to form letters – cars, baseballs, hands.

- Mount letters on another surface and cut around them to make a border for the word.

- Shadow letters – cut out two sets in different colors. Attach one set over the other with a little of the back one showing.

- Attach materials to letters – cotton balls for snow, beads, glitter.

- Pictures in letter shapes can take the place of letters or words. Put a tree in place of the word "tree."

The sign on the right was printed on the computer as a vertical banner and hung from the ceiling down to the display below.

- Use special fonts or clip art letters in computer programs, such as Print Shop. Enlarge each letter to fit on an 8-1/2 x 11 piece of paper and, if you have a color printer, print in color, or print in black on a colored piece of paper. Laminate and cut out.

- Use patterns for plain block letters, but trace and cut them from magazine pages that fit the theme. For example, cut letters for a sports display from a sports magazine or the sports section of the newspaper.

- Cut out two large letters, glue or staple the edges together and stuff with newspaper to make puffy letters that can be attached to a bulletin board or hung from the ceiling.

Letters and words are easier to apply and much more interesting if they are not mechanically straight. Letters should be placed optically so they are not perfect.

Place letters uphill, downhill, on a curve, jumbled, in a wave or bunched together to create interest. This works especially well if it fits with your theme. For example, use wavy letters for an oceanic theme.

ENLARGING DESIGNS

Graphics, shapes, and letters that you find are often not large enough to use on your bulletin board. There are several ways to enlarge items:

Photocopy machine

Many machines will enlarge items to 200% of their actual size. If your copy machine holds the large 11x17 paper, you can create large graphics for your board.

Though the ink color on copies is black, copying letters onto colored paper will create bright letters, especially those that are a style with empty space within the letter, such as outline or shadow.

Opaque projector

The opaque projector can take almost anything, such as a photo, a book, or a real object, and project that image on the wall. By moving the projector closer or farther from the wall you control the size of the image.

Overhead projector

Use the photocopy machine to make a clear transparency of the graphic. Then place this transparency on the overhead projector to project a much larger image on the wall. This is especially good for creating very large sized images.

Grid

This is the old fashioned, non-technology way to do it that takes a lot more time. Draw a small grid over the graphic. Place a larger grid on larger paper. Draw the larger image square by square. If your original grid is 1 inch square and your larger grid is 6 inches square you will increase the drawing to 6 times its original size.

3D BULLETIN BOARDS

Bulletin boards and displays are much more interesting if they are three dimensional. There are many ways you can make your displays extend off the flat surface:

- Bend or curve the letters or other materials.

- Use real items, such as hats, twigs, beads.

- Use materials with texture, such as bubble wrap, burlap, corrugated card board with the bumpy side out.

- Spacers – put foam, cardboard or other materials as a spacer behind letters or graphics so they stand out from the background.

- Overlap items.

- Bags or boxes can be attached to hold items.

- Use stuffed animals, toys or puppets.

- Twist or crumple paper – twisting brown paper to make a tree trunk, crumpling green paper to make a tree top or white paper to make a cloud.

- Cotton can be a cloud or snow.

- Double sided paper can be twisted to show two colors.

- Wood fence – made from real wooden pickets glued together or make a smaller version using craft sticks.

- Balloons, balls and other items.

INTERACTIVE BULLETIN BOARDS

Bulletin boards are not only passive learning tools, but can be designed and constructed to actively engage students.

Examples:
- Book Reviews – ask students to write reviews of books they like and post them or list books that need a boost in reading and ask for reviews.

- Quiz board – attach laminated paper flaps that can be lifted. Put a question on the top of the flap and the answer under the flap. The questions and answers can be changed periodically.

  A variation may have a question and the reference work where the answer can be found. The student looks up the answer and puts it into a box for a prize drawing.

- Boxes – attach small boxes to the board (like the ones Bandaids® are sold in). Label the boxes by genre, author or topic and put cards in each box listing a resource in the library in that category.

  Each box could also have a question on it with the cards in the box each listing a possible reference work. Students must choose the most appropriate reference work to use to answer the question.

RECYCLING AND REUSING BULLETIN BOARDS AND DISPLAYS

Displays should be functional and practical. When you have a bulletin board or display that you think works well, take a photo of it (Polaroid or digital cameras can provide an instant image).

Photograph the whole board and any individual pieces that you may need to remember when recreating the board at a later time.

Make notes about the theme and ideas for improving the display. Then file the photos along with pieces of the display to be used again.

Flat pieces that are going to be used year after year can be laminated and attached to the background with Velcro or double sided tape.

STORAGE

Bulletin board materials take up a lot of space when stored for future use. Some ideas for storage of the materials:

- Large resealable plastic bags can hold many materials, label by the theme or topic, include a photo of the board and notes about assembly.

- Resealable plastic bags can also be used to store letters and words, label with the content.

- Artist portfolio cases can hold large, flat pieces.

- Large flat map drawers

- Butcher paper can be folded around the materials to form a large envelope, taped shut, labeled and stored.

THEMES AND IDEAS

- Create a perpetual calendar by drawing a monthly grid on a large sheet of railroad board, with separate numbers, 1-31, that can be attached using velcro.

The weather calendar has numbers for each day and symbols for the type of weather. Both are attached with Velcro.

- What I Read on My Summer Vacation – staff or students choose books that they read, display with beach umbrella, sunglasses, airplane boarding passes.

- Calendar related items – Girl Scout Week, holidays, seasons, and observances.

- Summertime and the Reading is Easy – teddy bear in a string hammock hanging between two trees with good summer reads.

- Spring cleaning – books that are gathering dust, include a feather duster and furniture polish in display.

- Got the Blues? or Red Hot Books – focus on a color (school colors?), include books with the color in the title, or that color on their cover.

- How do you do it? – use with how-to and craft books. Include craft materials and tools in the display.

- Countdown – this can be a countdown to anything – summer vacation, New Year's, Dr. Seuss's birthday, or an event at the school. Use clear plastic book pockets to hold cards to show how many days it is to the event. Make it a surprise event by including facts and hints and see if students can guess what it is.

- Who's who?– Include portraits of people that are represented in your biography collection. Have a contest asking students to find out who's represented on the bulletin board by searching the library.

RESOURCES

Books:

Bulletin Boards, Displays and Special Events for School Libraries. Santa Barbara, CA: ABC-CLIO, 1991.

Feldshuh, Muriel, *Flip-Up Bulletin Boards: A Step-By-Step Guide to Creating Hands-On Cross-Curricular Bulletin Boards All Year Long.* Jefferson City, MO: Scholastic Professional Books, 1996.

Forte, Imogene, *Easy-To-Make and Use Library and Reference Bulletin Boards.* Nashville, TN: Incentive Publications, 1986.

Hawthorne, Karen and Jane E. Gibson, *Bulletin Boards and 3-D Showcases That Capture Them with Pizzazz.* Englewood, CO: Libraries Unlimited, 1999.

Norby, Shirley, *Media Center Bulletin Boards: Bulletin Boards, Book Displays, Book Lists, and Literature-Based Activities.* Grand Rapid, MI: TS Denison, 1996.

Vansgard, Amy, *Simply Super Bulletin Boards.* Ft. Atkinson, WI: Alleyside Press (an imprint of Highsmith Press), 1997.

Wollner, Elizabeth Shelton, *Literature-Based Bulletin Boards, Grades K-2: Create Interactive Bulletin Boards That Turn Into Beautiful Big Books - Instantly!* New York: Scholastic Professional Books, 1997.

The entrance to the Doris Dillon Library at Graystone Elementary School in San Jose Unified School District is colorful and welcoming. The picket fences, flowers and the many displays of books, posters and other resources make it a treat for the eyes.

PR & MARKETING

Public relations (PR) is used to describe a broad effort to create an overall favorable opinion about something.

Formal public relations happens through a planned effort to:
- Improve relations;
- Create favorable opinion;
- Generate support.

Informal public relations happens in the daily interactions between the library staff and your customers (students, teachers, parents and others who come into contact with your library and its services).

Marketing has a more specific focus related to "selling" a product or a service and involves a number of activities including:
- Advertising;
- Shipping/delivery; and
- Selling.

Who is your public?

Begin planning for public relations by first identifying your public – those groups that you serve or wish to reach with information about your library media center. In the business world these groups of people are referred to as "customers."

Publics can be identified in two groups:

- **Internal** – those groups of people within the family of education, the school, or directly associated with the library.

  Internal groups might include students, teachers, classified staff (custodians, clerks, and secretaries), administrators, district office staff, or school board members.

- **External** – those groups of people who are outside of the family of education and the school or have indirect relationships with the school library.

  External groups might include parents, community members, business people, publishers, authors, or vendors.

> LIBRARY QUOTE:
>
> *A library is not a luxury but one of the necessities of life.*
>
> Henry Ward Beecher

Here are two examples of specific "publics" and some possible answers to these three questions.

Faculty members:
Why communicate?
- To form a positive opinion of the library and its services.
- To get them to use the library more.

What do they need to know?
- What is in the library.
- How the library can support them in their teaching.

How to communicate?
- One-on-one, visit them in the staff room or in their classroom.
- Introduce yourself and find out what units they are planning.
- Show them what you have that might work for their students.
- Bring new books and booktalk them to the class.

- Have a "morning in the media center" and serve coffee and goodies before school with invitations issued to the faculty and have new books and resources on display.

Board members:
Why communicate?
- So they know you and the library exist.
- Help them to value the library's role in education.

What do they need to know?
- That the library is used by students and teachers.
- That the library fills a valuable role in student achievement.

How to communicate?
- Shower them with invitations to come to read books to students, to events, celebrations and presentations, especially when the presentation features student work accomplished through the library.
- Welcome them when they come, show them how students are using the library and its resources.
- Include information about the use of the library, how many students visit weekly, how many books are checked out, etc.

Attitudes and Opinions

It is important to know how to influence your customers/publics. Attitudes and opinions are created through a combination of ways and are constantly reinforced.

How do people form attitudes?

1. **Personal experiences**
   The most powerful way in which an attitude is formed is through one's own personal experience.

   If a teacher or a student comes into your library and is ignored or left wandering around without being helped, they may form a negative attitude about the library. If they feel welcome and are promptly helped, they may form a positive attitude about the library.

2. **Personal experience of others you trust**
   The next most powerful way an attitude is formed is through believing other people's experiences. That's why the advertising world is filled with testimonials by famous, trustworthy people. That's also why we read reviews of books or movies, because we trust the reviewer's opinions.

   If a teacher or a popular student feels that the library is a great place to go, their friends may believe it also, even if they have never been in the library.

3. **Advertising**
   Posters, newsletters and other types of advertising have some influence on people's attitudes, but these methods must be continually reinforced.

Someone who already has a positive attitude about the library may pay more attention to print materials about the library.

4. **Reports and studies**
   Scholarly reports, research, studies, data are all used to influence opinions.

   The popularity of publications such as *Consumer Reports* illustrates how people use studies to form opinions about products with which they do not have personal experience.

Attitudes, once formed, are very difficult to change. Remember that each time you interact with someone you are helping them to form an attitude about you and the library in which you work.

WHAT YOU CAN DO

Remember that daily interactions help to form attitudes and opinions, so SMILE!

Welcome students and staff to your library. Find out what they need and want and try to fill those needs.

Strong Library Program

Remember that effective public relations starts with a strong library program. This can be stated as:

Performance + Recognition = Public Relations

Ask yourself:
1. Is the collection adequate, curriculum - oriented, and well rounded?

43

2. Are the physical facilities attractive, comfortable and reasonably spacious?

3. Is your budget sufficient to carry out more than a bare minimum of service and activities?

4. Are you and/or your staff professionally trained, enthusiastic, and competent?

5. Do you have a planned and scheduled PR program?

For a more comprehensive assessment of your library program see *Check It Out! Assessing School Library Media Programs: A Guide for School District Education Policy and Implementation Teams.* This guide was produced by the California Department of Education to assist districts in assessing their programs.

Data and Information

Information and research results on school libraries are included on pages 45-57.

These pages may be copied onto overhead transparencies for presentations, included in newsletter articles or posted in your library.

RESOURCES:

Internet:
Library Research Service, Colorado State Library
http://www.lrs.org/
Summaries of several research studies on school libraries conducted by Keith Curry Lance are available at this site.

Books:

California Department of Education, *Check It Out! Assessing School Library Media Programs: A Guide for School District Education Policy and Implementation Teams.* Sacramento, CA: California Department of Education, 1998.

Hartzell, Gary N, *Building Influence for the School Librarian.* Worthington, OH: Linworth Publishing, Inc., 1994.

Krashen, Stephen, *The Power of Reading: Insights From the Research.* Englewood, CO: Libraries Unlimited, 1993.

Lance, Keith Curry, et a,. *How School Librarians Help Kids Achieve Standards: The Second Colorado Study.* San Jose, CA: Hi Willow Research & Publishing, 2000.

Lance, Keith Curry, et al, *Information Empowered: The School Librarian as an Agent of Academic Achievement in Alaska Schools.* Juneau, AK: Alaska State Library, 1999.

Tips and Other Bright Ideas for School Librarians. Santa Barbara, CA: ABC-CLIO, 1991.

Valenza, Joyce Kasman, *Power Tools: 100+ Essential Forms and Presentations for Your School Library Information Program.* Chicago, IL: American Library Association, 1998.

Zweizig, Douglas, et al, *Lessons From Library Power: Enriching Teaching and Learning: Final Report of the National Library Power Initiative.* Englewood, CO: Libraries Unlimited, 1999.

SCHOOL LIBRARY COLLECTIONS

- Average number of library books per student:

Elementary	21
Middle School	15
High School	17

- Total average (mean) expenditures per student on collections:

Elementary	$28.57
Middle School	$21.97
High School	$42.94

Data from Miller, Marilyn and Marilyn Shontz. "How do You Measure Up? Expenditures for Resources in School Library Media Centers, 1997-98" School Library Journal, October 1999, pages 50-59.

SCHOOL LIBRARY STAFFING

- Average number of pupils per library media specialist is 870.

- Average number of schools that have state certified library media specialists:

Elementary	47%
Secondary	49%

- Average levels of state certified library media specialists per school:

Elementary	.8 FTE
Secondary	1.1 FTE

Data from National Center for Education Statistics, *School Library Media Centers: 1993-94.* Washington, DC: U.S. Department of Education, 1998. Tables A-11, A-13, A-15.

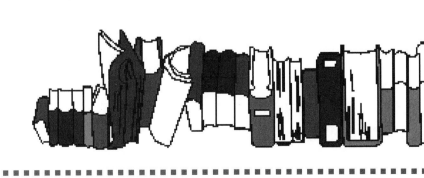

SCHOOL LIBRARY MISSION

The mission of the school library media center is to ensure that students and staff are effective users of ideas and information.

This mission is accomplished:

- by providing intellectual and physical access to materials in all formats;

- by providing instruction to foster competence and stimulate interest in reading, viewing, and using information and ideas;

- by working with other educators to design learning strategies to meet the needs of individual students.

American Association of School Librarians and the Association for Educational Communications and Technology, *Information Power: Building Partnerships for Learning.* Chicago, IL: American Library Association, 1998

Research Results...

THE COLORADO STUDY

- A US Department of Education study in Colorado found "among school and community predictors of academic achievement, the size of the library media center staff and collection is second only to the absence of at-risk conditions, particularly poverty and low educational attainment among adults."

- When controlled for these social and economic differences, they found that "students at schools with better funded library media centers have higher than average test scores, whether their schools and communities are rich or poor and whether adults in the community are well or poorly educated."

Lance, Keith Curry,, *The Impact of School Library Media Centers on Academic Achievement.* San Jose, CA: Hi Willow Research, 1993

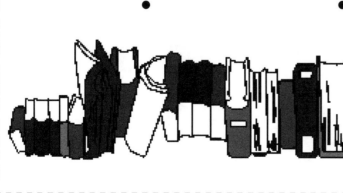

Research Results...

THE SECOND COLORADO STUDY

A second study of the schools in Colorado found that:

- "Colorado Student Assessment Program (CSAP) reading scores increase with increases in the following characteristics of library media (LM) programs:
  - LM program development
  - information technology
  - teacher/library media specialist (LMS) collaboration
  - individual visits to the library media center (LMC)."

- "Test scores rise in both elementary and middle schools as library media specialists and teachers work together."

Lance, Keith Curry, et al, *How School Librarians Help Kids Achieve Standards: The Second Colorado Study*. San Jose, CA: Hi Willow Research, 2000.

Research Results...

THE ALASKA STUDY

This study identified several positive, statistically significant relationships between characteristics of school library media programs and academic achievement by students.

- Where there is a librarian, test scores are higher.

- Generally, a school with a full-time librarian is likely to have higher test scores than a school with no librarian.

- The more often students receive library/information literacy instruction in which library media staff are involved, the higher the test scores.

Lance, Keith Curry, et al. *Information Empowered: The School Librarian as an Agent of Academic Achievement in Alaska Schools.* Juneau, Alaska: Alaska State Library, 1999. Page 66.

Research Results...

THE POWER OF READING

This book is a survey of many research studies related to reading. Some of the findings include:

- Children in schools with no library read half as much as children in schools with libraries.

- Children who had access to school libraries read more than students with access only to classroom collections of books.

- Numerous studies show, "more reading results in better reading comprehension, writing style, vocabulary, spelling, and grammatical development."

Krashen, Stephen. *The Power of Reading: Insights from the Research.* Englewood, CO: Libraries Unlimited. 1993.

COLLECTION DEVELOPMENT

Delivering
the right information
to the right person
at the right time,
in the right place,
in the right format,
using the best technology delivery system
is the vision of the collection development plan.

David V. Loertscher and Blanche Woolls
in *Building a School Library Collection Plan*

Collection development involves four major activities that are interdependent and continuously interacting:

- Identification of your library's customers and their needs and interests.
- Understanding of your library's mission and the curriculum of the school.
- Identification of what doesn't belong in the collection and weeding it out.
- Selection of the best materials to meet the needs and gaps in your collection.

This interactive process is represented by the following graphic:

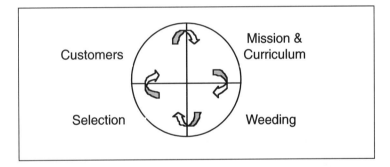

Customers

You need to understand your customers – who uses your library? Students at what grade level? What languages do they speak? What reading level are they? What are their interests? Do you serve staff? What are their needs?

Curriculum/Mission

What should you have in your library? What is the purpose of your library? What curriculum is taught at your school? What are students expected to know? What teaching strategies are used that may require library resources?

Weeding

What doesn't fit with your mission? What materials don't belong in your library? Where are the gaps in your collection?

Selection

How will you choose what to put into your collection? What tools will you use? What criteria will you apply?

COLLECTION CONTENT

Building a library collection that best serves the students and staff requires a knowledge of:
- the library mission, and
- the curriculum taught at the school.

Library Mission

The mission of the library media program is to ensure that students and staff are effective users of ideas and information. The major purposes of the school library are to support the curriculum and foster reading and literacy in all students.

The school library is not supposed to be the preserver of all knowledge and keeper of all materials nor is it supposed to serve all members of the community. The school library serves the students and staff of the school (and maybe the students' parents).

The school library does not have a balanced collection, that is, it doesn't have something about every topic. The school library's collection is focused on the curriculum taught at the school and the needs and interests of its students.

Curriculum

There are several ways to find out what the curriculum is at your school.

To find out what is taught now:

1. **Survey**
   Send a brief form to every teacher each month asking what topics or units they will be teaching next month in their class. As you gather these over the course of a year, you'll be able to see what is being taught now at your school

and when in the year it is taught (see the sample form on page 67).

2. **District curriculum maps or guides**
   Many districts have developed curriculum guides that give the major topics and units of study for each grade level and for each subject. They may also have information on the specific projects and research that students are expected to do.

   Some districts have condensed these guides into a single page that lists the topics and skills that will be covered in that class. Often these are distributed to parents at the start of the year.

3. **Textbook series**
   Look at the textbooks that are used at your school to see what kinds of topics, projects and recommended readings are included.

To find out what should be taught:
You need to look at two sets of documents that are very important in schools, frameworks and standards.

1. Frameworks

Most state departments of education have adopted curriculum frameworks in major subject areas, for grades K-12. Each framework usually includes research on that subject, suggestions for teaching strategies, themes, strands and the specific content that should be taught at each grade level and the criteria that will be used to adopt instructional materials.

Frameworks may also include the state content and performance standards, if they have been adopted for that subject area. The framework can be a useful tool to

© 2001 Santa Clara County Office of Education

determine what topics and information you need to have in your library.

For example, the *History-Social Science Framework for California, 1997* edition, includes the following for grade four:

> *Missions, Ranchos, and the Mexican War for Independence*
>
> *One reason for settling California was to bring Christianity to the native peoples. Students should understand the geographical factors involved in locating the missions so that they were a day's walk apart and situated along native pathways near sources of water. Presidios were erected by the colonial governors on sites that could be defended. Cattle ranches and agricultural villages were developed around the missions and presidios. European plants, agriculture, and a herding economy were introduced to the region.*
>
> *To bring the history of this period to life, teachers should emphasize the daily lives of the people who occupied the ranchos, missions, presidios, haciendas, and pueblos. Reading literature; making field trips to a mission or early California home; singing songs; and dramatizing a rodeo, fiesta, or trading day when Yankee clipper ships arrived to trade for California hides and tallow will bring this period alive.*

This small portion of the framework includes many topics and suggestions for library resources, including:
- geography;
- rodeos and fiestas;
- clipper ships;
- trade;
- agriculture.

It also describes the detailed information about missions that is needed, namely:
- where they were located and why;
- the daily lives of people living in and around the mission; and
- the changes that happened as a result of the mission.

These are all topics that should be a part of your library's collection if your school has students in grade four.

If teachers are going to dramatize a rodeo or fiesta, your library should have information on these events including:
- what activities took place;
- what food was served;
- who attended, and;
- what music was played.

WHAT YOU CAN DO

Look at the frameworks for the grade levels in your school for clues to help you in your collection development.

---

2. Standards

Most states have adopted content and performance standards in the basic curriculum areas of science, mathematics, reading-language arts and history-social science. Content standards state what students should know while performance standards indicate how that knowledge will be demonstrated.

These state standards are often the basis for the adoption of instructional materials and are also used for statewide testing of student achievement. Schools throughout the nation are aligning their curriculum and the instructional materials they use with their state standards.

These standards may include topics that may not have been taught before or were previously taught at a different grade level. Your library collection needs to have resources to support teachers as they make this shift to teach the content included in your state standards.

The standards may also provide examples of activities that students may engage in or research that they might conduct.

The Indiana Social Studies Proficiency Guide: An Aid to Curriculum Development, 1996 edition, includes the following:

FOCUS: INDIANA IN THE NATION AND THE WORLD

GEOGRAPHIC RELATIONSHIPS

Demonstrate an understanding of Indiana's geographical relationship to the nation and the world.

Proficiency Statements and Indicators
Students should be able to:

• *Identify and classify natural resources, show their worldwide distribution patterns, and recognize the physical and human limits on the use of resources.*

• *Describe and compare urban and rural communities in Indiana and other regions of the world and explain their interdependence.*

• *Make simple maps to show how communities in Indiana are linked together by movement of people, ideas and products.*

Sample Student Activities
Students might:

• *Choose food product with numerous resources (ingredients) listed on the label. Determine the origins of these resources and indicate findings on a world map.*

• *Make charts listing the types of businesses and industries found in rural and urban areas. Draw arrows between industries that depend upon each other in some way.*

• *Creat overlay maps drawn on clear acetate which show transportation systems (trails, canals, roads) of the past and present.*

page 59

This portion of Indiana's standards includes several topics and suggestions for library resources that may not have been a part of your library collection, including:

• food products and their origins;
• industries and businesses and their suppliers;
• historical forms of transportation; and
• historical maps.

WHAT YOU CAN DO

Skim through the frameworks and standards documents for your state. Note the topics and the types of materials and resources that you should have in your collection. Also look for suggested activities that depend on the library – research reports, reading requirements, or interdisciplinary activities. See the list of web sites for state standards on pages 65-66.

COLLECTION REVIEW

Once you have identified a list of topics that you should have in your library you will need to determine where the gaps are in your collection.

After you have weeded out the materials that are damaged, outdated or no longer relevant to your library, you need to compare your list of topics with the materials currently in your collection to develop a list of library purchase needs. A sample form is provided on page 69.

Don't forget to include the recreational reading needs and interests of your students in your purchase needs.

WHAT YOU CAN DO

On the Library Holdings and Purchase Needs form (see sample on page 69) list the topics that you should have in your collection and note the grade level(s) that would use these materials the most. Keep in mind the various reading and ability levels of the students who will use these materials.

Then check your library catalog to see what you have on these topics, include both books (fiction and nonfiction) and other types of materials.

If you find that you have nothing or that your collection is not sufficient, note your purchase needs.

If your library catalog is automated, you may be able to print out a list with the numbers of titles in your library by call number. This list can help you get an overview of your total collection to see what you have in the various Dewey categories as well as in fiction and easy readers or other special collections. Also review the holdings for copyright date to see where your collection may need updating.

HAVE A PLAN

It is important to have a plan for what you will purchase for the library. When you review the collection you may find that you have more resources in certain areas and fewer resources in other areas. Without a plan the collection may only reflect the personal interests of the library staff or of the teachers and students who use the library the most.

However, it may not meet the needs of the total curriculum or the needs of those students and teachers who don't use the library as often.

Before looking for materials to purchase, decide on the types of materials and topics needed in the library collection. Refer to this "shopping list" when you are visiting exhibits, reviewing publisher's catalogs, or searching in library selection tools. This list can keep you focused and help you resist impulse buying.

RESOURCES

Internet:
See the page 65-66 for state standards on the Internet.

Books:

Doll, Carol Ann and Pamela Petrick Barron, *Collection Analysis for the School Library Media Center: A Practical Approach.* Chicago, IL: American Library Association, 1991.

Loertscher, David and Blanche Woolls, *Building a School Library Collection Plan: A Beginning Handbook.* San Jose, CA: Hi Willow Research, 1998.

Thomson, Elizabeth, *Reference and Collection Development on the Internet.* New York: Neal-Schuman Publishers, 1996.

STATE STANDARDS ON THE INTERNET

Alabama
http://www.alsde.edu

Alaska
http://www.educ.state.ak.us/ContentStandards/

Arizona
http://www.ade.state.az.us/standards/

Arkansas
http://arkedu.state.ar.us/standard.htm

California
http://www.cde.ca.gov/board/

Colorado
http://www.cde.state.co.us/index_stnd.htm

Connecticut
http://www.state.ct.us/sde/dtl/curriculum/index.htm

Delaware
http://www.doe.state.de.us/DPIServices/
DOE_Standards.htm

Florida
http://www.firn.edu/doe/menu/sss.htm

Georgia
http://www.glc.k12.ga.us/

Hawaii
http://www.hcps.k12.hi.us/

Idaho
http://www.sde.state.id.us/osbe/exstand.htm

Illinois
http://www.isbe.state.il.us/ils/

Indiana
http://ideanet.doe.state.in.us/standards/

Iowa
(standards locally determined by districts)

Kansas
http://www.ksbe.state.ks.us/assessment/

Kentucky
http://www.kde.state.ky.us/oapd/curric/

Louisiana
http://www.lcet.doe.state.la.us/conn/

Maine
http://janus.state.me.us/education/lres/lres.htm

Maryland
http://mdk12.org/mspp/standards/

Massachusetts
http://www.doe.mass.edu/frameworks/current.html

Michigan
http://cdp.mde.state.mi.us/MCF/ContentStandards/

Minnesota
http://cfl.state.mn.us/GRAD/highstandards.htm

Mississippi
http://www.mde.k12.ms.us/curriculum/

Missouri
http://www.dese.state.mo.us/standards/

Montana
http://www.metnet.state.mt.us/SchoolImprovement/
HTM/Mtstandards.shtml

Nebraska
http://www.edneb.org/IPS/Issu/AcadStand.html

Nevada
http://www.nde.state.nv.us/sca/standards/index.html

New Hampshire
http://www.ed.state.nh.us/CurriculumFrameworks/
curricul.htm

New Jersey
http://www.state.nj.us/njded/stass/

New Mexico
http://www.sde.state.nm.us/

New York
http://www.emsc.nysed.gov/ciai/pub.html

North Carolina
http://www.dpi.state.nc.us/curriculum/

North Dakota
http://www.dpi.state.nd.us/standard/

Ohio
http://www.ode.state.oh.us/ca/ci/

Oklahoma
http://www.sde.state.ok.us/publ/pass.html

Oregon
http://www.ode.state.or.us/cimcam/
academicStandards.htm

Pennsylvania
http://www.pde.psu.edu/standard/stan.html

Rhode Island
http://www.ridoe.net/standards/frameworks/

South Carolina
http://www.sde.state.sc.us/sde/test123/
standard.htm

South Dakota
http://www.state.sd.us/deca/ContentStandards/
index.htm

Tennessee
http://www.state.tn.us/education/ci/
cicurframwkmain.htm

Texas
http://www.tea.state.tx.us/teks/

Utah
http://www.uen.org/curriculum/

Vermont
http://www.state.vt.us/educ/stand/framework.htm

Virginia
http://www.pen.k12.va.us/VDOE/Instruction/sol.html

Washington
http://www.k12.wa.us/reform/frameworks/
framework.asp

West Virginia
http://wvde.state.wv.us/igos/

Wisconsin
http://www.dpi.state.wi.us/dpi/standards/

Wyoming
http://www.k12.wy.us/publications/standards.html

FROM YOUR SCHOOL LIBRARY

Please help me support your classroom lessons with library activities and resources by letting me know what your focus is for the month of: _____

Thanks

TO: _____

ROOM: _____

READING-LANGUAGE ARTS

_____

_____

_____

SCIENCE

_____

_____

_____

OTHER SUBJECTS

_____

_____

_____

HISTORY-SOCIAL SCIENCE

_____

_____

_____

MATHEMATICS

_____

_____

_____

Any other comments?

_____

_____

_____

67

Library Holdings and Purchase Needs

Enter the topics you have identified that need to be included in your library and grade level(s) that are most applicable. Search your catalog for current holdings (best done after major weeding has occurred). Note those topics for which you should purchase materials.

TOPIC	GRADE	LIBRARY HOLDINGS			PURCHASE?
		Fiction	NonFiction	Other	

WEEDING

A garden needs weeding in order for it to be productive and to allow the flowers and vegetables to grow. Your library needs to be weeded to be more productive. Removing the old, unattractive, outdated materials allows your new resources to shine.

There are two major processes in library collection development:
- acquiring materials, and
- getting rid of materials.

Because there has traditionally been a scarcity of library resources, many people have been reluctant to remove resources from the library, but the process can be viewed as the opposite, and necessary, part of selection, that is de-selection.

Why Weed?

- No room for new materials to be shelved – space is not used efficiently.

- Collection is outdated, unused and unattractive because of old materials.

- Shelves full of materials give the illusion of a good library collection – it doesn't show a need for new materials.

- Maintaining unneeded materials is time consuming and unproductive.

- To provide the best possible service through a quality collection.

- To correct mistakes in selection.

There are several published criteria that are used when evaluating whether something should be removed from a library. However, many of them were not developed specifically for school libraries.

Criteria for Weeding School Libraries

When it comes to weeding, we want to **C-U-DO-IT**!

C	=	curriculum fit
U	=	use
D	=	damage
O	=	outdated information
I	=	interest levels/reading levels
T	=	too many copies

These criteria were developed for school libraries. Think of these criteria when you are trying to determine whether you should de-select (weed) something from your school library.

Curriculum fit

The materials do not fit the current curriculum taught at the school. The mission of the school library is to support the curriculum and the recreational reading needs of the students, not to preserve historical documents or to have comprehensive collections in all areas.

Use

The materials have not been used or checked out for some time. Why are they unused? Materials that are cataloged incorrectly or have unattractive covers might be used if those factors were corrected. Are media materials no longer used because there is no appropriate equipment or the medium is outdated?

NOTE: Do not use this as the sole reason for removing an item from your collection.

Damaged

The materials are so damaged or worn out that they are not usable. You must decide whether to repair, replace or remove them.

Outdated information

Some or all of the content is out-of-date and incorrect. This is especially important in the areas of science, health, geography and current affairs, where information changes frequently. Does it have stereotypes or reflect biased viewpoints? Also check science experiments or craft books for unsafe procedures or use of toxic materials.

Interest levels

The interest or reading levels are not appropriate for the students at your school. Have the grade levels or student population changed at your school? The format may not fit the interests of the students – is the print too small, are the illustrations of poor quality, is the layout difficult to read?

Too many copies

The title may once have been more popular, but due to changes (in curriculum or student interest) fewer copies are needed now.

Procedures for Weeding

1. Establish a weeding plan, schedule or goal:
   • Plan to do a set time each day, week or month.
   • Decide to weed a particular collection or Dewey area.
   • Write out your plan and make a commitment.

2. Weed when you have few interruptions:
   • Before or after the school day.
   • When no classes or students are scheduled in the library.
   • During special assemblies or early inservice days.

3. Assemble a weeding kit that includes:
   • Notebook to keep track of what areas have been weeded.
   • Gloves or other protection from dust.
   • Bookmarks (see page 75) or sticky notes to note reasons for removal from shelf.
   • Box for books that need repair.
   • Cart or box for books that will be discarded.

4. Pull each book from the shelf and examine it using your criteria:
   • Check the copyright date.
   • Check the physical condition of the book.
   • Examine the contents of the book, check the index and any section labeled "today" or the "future" – this is often where it is easiest to find out if the content is outdated.

5. Decide what to do and put the book
   • Back on the shelf, or
   • Note the reasons and place the book either in the repair box or the discard stack.

6. Note where you started and stopped in your notebook or mark the shelf.

   Note: Sometimes you may want to "sleep on" your decision to remove some books. These can be placed in a holding area for a period of time and reviewed again at a later date by yourself, a teacher, or other library staff for concurrence with the decision to discard.

Removing Materials

Check your school/district policy on removal of materials. Some districts require a list of materials and Board approval before discarding. Some policies may require offering materials to teachers, students or their families. Some funding sources may have requirements before discarding materials purchased with those funds. Be aware of any restrictions or requirements before you move forward.

Catalog Records

A. Automated catalogs
This process is easier and often involves only one step, removing the item or that copy of the item from the on-line catalog data base. Each system has its own procedures for doing this. Refer to your automation manual for details.

If you maintain a manual shelf list, pull the card and make a notation as to which copy was weeded and the date. If all of the copies were weeded, make the notation and put the shelf list card for that title in a separate location.

B. Card Catalogs

1. Find the shelf list card for each item you have weeded.
   - If the book is a single copy, mark it discarded and date it.
   - If there are multiple copies, note which copy was discarded and date it.

2. Pull all the catalog cards for items where all copies are being discarded. This includes the cards for the author, title, subject, series, etc. Mark each card as you pull it – drawing a line through the printed information is sufficient. This is to prevent you from inadvertently filing that card back again.

3. Pull the circulation card from the item(s).

4. Bundle all cards for the same item together (shelf list, catalog and circulation card).

5. File them together for a year (a shoe box works well). Label it with the year of discard.

6. Count how many books and other materials you have weeded. This is good data to have to show how much outdated and inappropriate material was in the library and to show the need for buying new materials to replace those discarded.

   It is also useful to keep track of the publication date of the materials you discard. Simply putting a tick mark on a sheet divided by year or by decade is sufficient. You are less likely to get criticism for discarding materials when you can show how very outdated they are.

Removing Materials

1. Pull out the circulation cards and pockets.

2. Cross out all school identification. If you don't, those books will find their way back to your library, sometimes many years later.

3. Stamp or write "DISCARDED" on the inside cover and title page and remove or put a mark through the bar code.

4. Remove the books from the library. How you do this will depend on your school policy.

   Some options are:

   • Allow teachers and students to take materials, if content is still usable.

   • One librarian keeps a "Still Good Books" box in the library for the students in her school to take and keep. Many of the students come from poor homes and have no books of their own.

   • Donate the materials that are still current and usable to nonprofit groups.

   • Throw away or recycle those that are outdated or damaged.

     Remember, bad information is worse than no information. Children in classrooms, private schools or in thirdworld countries don't need outdated information either.

   • Sell items that may have value to return funds to the library.

If you are giving away discarded books you may want in insert a bookmark (see page 77) to explain the reasons why the books are being discarded.

WHAT YOU CAN DO

Weeding is also a political process. Teachers or parents may be upset that you are "throwing away perfectly good books," because they don't understand what you are doing.

Prepare your principal and teachers and in advance. Show them an old book on a topic beside a new book and ask them which they want their students to have. Point out the misinformation in the materials being weeded and clearly communicate the criteria you are using to weed the collection.

RESOURCES

Internet:

Sunlink Weed of the Month Club
http://www.sunlink.ucf.edu/weed/
This site provides Florida's School Library Media Specialists with guidelines and suggestions for weeding their collections.

Books:

Boon, Belinda, *The CREW Method: Expanded Guidelines for Collection Evaluation and Weeding for Small and Medium-Sized Public Libraries.* Austin, TX: Texas State Library, 1995.

Slote, Stanley G., *Weeding Library Collections: Library Weeding Methods.* Englewood, CO: Libraries Unlimited, 1997.

DIRECTIONS: Photocopy and cut apart. Use these bookmarks to note reasons for possible discard of a book.

POSSIBLE DISCARD	**POSSIBLE DISCARD**	**POSSIBLE DISCARD**
Check reasons and note examples and page numbers.	Check reasons and note examples and page numbers.	Check reasons and note examples and page numbers.
☐ Damaged beyond repair	☐ Damaged beyond repair	☐ Damaged beyond repair
☐ Another copy on shelf	☐ Another copy on shelf	☐ Another copy on shelf
☐ Replace this title	☐ Replace this title	☐ Replace this title
☐ Outdated information	☐ Outdated information	☐ Outdated information
☐ Unattractive	☐ Unattractive	☐ Unattractive
☐ Doesn't fit curriculum	☐ Doesn't fit curriculum	☐ Doesn't fit curriculum
☐ Bias/Stereotypes	☐ Bias/Stereotypes	☐ Bias/Stereotypes
☐ Newer materials in library	☐ Newer materials in library	☐ Newer materials in library
☐ Not used	☐ Not used	☐ Not used
☐ Age/Reading level not appropriate	☐ Age/Reading level not appropriate	☐ Age/Reading level not appropriate
Other comments:	Other comments:	Other comments:
Initials: Date:	Initials: Date:	Initials: Date:

DIRECTIONS: Photocopy and cut apart. Place these bookmarks in discarded books that will be given away to explain why they are being discarded.

DISCARDED MATERIALS

Though this item may appear to be useful, it has been removed from the library for one or more of the following reasons:

- It is outdated or inaccurate

- It has bias or stereotypes

- It doesn't support the curriculum currently taught at this school

- Better, newer titles are available

- Other copies are still available in the library

- It is damaged

We strive to provide the best library resources for our students.

De-selecting materials is an essential part of the process.

DISCARDED MATERIALS

Though this item may appear to be useful, it has been removed from the library for one or more of the following reasons:

- It is outdated or inaccurate

- It has bias or stereotypes

- It doesn't support the curriculum currently taught at this school

- Better, newer titles are available

- Other copies are still available in the library

- It is damaged

We strive to provide the best library resources for our students.

De-selecting materials is an essential part of the process.

DISCARDED MATERIALS

Though this item may appear to be useful, it has been removed from the library for one or more of the following reasons:

- It is outdated or inaccurate

- It has bias or stereotypes

- It doesn't support the curriculum currently taught at this school

- Better, newer titles are available

- Other copies are still available in the library

- It is damaged

We strive to provide the best library resources for our students.

De-selecting materials is an essential part of the process.

SELECTION

Just as a person shopping for holiday presents for friends and family develops a plan – how much to spend, what kinds of gifts to buy for whom, where and when to shop – you need to develop a plan for improving your collection.

After you have:
- identified your customers (students and staff);
- assessed the curriculum (what is taught now and what should be taught);
- weeded out the materials that don't belong (or at least a large number of them);
- determined what you currently have in your library;

you are ready to identify the gaps and to build your purchase wish list. Then, with your plan in hand, you can begin to look for the resources you need.

WHAT YOU CAN DO

Before selecting and purchasing materials, review your district's selection policy. Many districts require that all library purchases be approved by the district Library Coordinator or another library professional. See the chapter on Library Policies for more detailed information.

Selection Resources

There are many good selection resources that have reviews of books and other materials and recommendations for purchase. Some of these resources are fairly expensive and you may not have them at each school. Check with your district office or county office of education for selection resources you may use.

Several print and Internet selection resources are listed at the end of this chapter. Other good sources are publications by professional associations such as the American Library Association, and the International Reading Association.

Children's choice award lists, such as the California Young Reader Medal, feature books that have been reviewed and chosen by students as their favorites.

Selection Criteria

Selection of quality library materials is a complex process. Both the quality of the materials themselves and how they fit with the needs of your library and your students must be considered.

A brief summary of criteria to look at when evaluating fiction and nonfiction books follows on page 81-82.

WHAT YOU CAN DO

Review the criteria. Then examine several books now in your library and see if they fit the criteria listed.

No handbook can provide the breadth and depth of information and experience needed to do a good job of selecting materials. If you have not had the training or experience to feel comfortable making your own choices, use the selection and review sources available to you. Also try to work together with the teachers at your school and the library staff at other schools in your district. Your collection will benefit and your job will be easier if you combine your efforts and share information across the district.

See the list starting on page 83 for some suggested resources.

Making Decisions

Remember that even though the selection resources listed will provide a starting place for your selection efforts, these resources aren't the only way to find books and materials for your library.

Visit the exhibits at conferences and materials fairs. Look at the items on display and collect catalogs from publishers and jobbers. Bring your purchase list and ask the salespeople if they have titles that meet your most pressing needs.

Don't be swayed by the title or a flashy cover – look through the contents to be sure it covers what you need and is at the appropriate reading and interest level.

If the item fits your library needs, be sure to add it to your consideration/purchase file. See the chapter on PURCHASING for more information.

FICTION BOOKS

Basic
No bias for race or gender
Universality, ageless appeal
Originality

Values
Vitality
Charming
Distinctive

Plot
Does the book tell a story?
Does the plot have action and suspense?
Is it convincing?
Is the plot well constructed?
Is it dramatic?

Content
Is the story worth telling?
Is it an appropriate story for the audience?
How might it fit into the curriculum?
Is the ending consistent with the theme?

Theme
What is the theme?
Is the theme worth writing about?
Is the theme a natural part of the story?
Does the book avoid moralizing?

Format
Is the appearance of the book attractive?
Do the illustrations add to the story?
Is the print clear and readable?
Does the book have a durable binding?

Characterization
Are the characters convincing and believable?
Is the description of the characters vivid and clear?
Does the reader see the character's strengths and their weaknesses?
Is there any character development or growth?

Style
Is the story represented clearly with simplicity and directness?
Do the characters speak in a natural way?
Do the descriptions add beauty and understanding to the story?
Does the author avoid overused words and ideas?
Does the book show real individuality?

Other considerations
How does the book compare with other books on the same subject?
How does the book compare with other books by the same author?
Will this book fill a need in the library collection?

Compiled by Alice Bethke, Santa Clara Unified School District, from several sources.

NONFICTION BOOKS

Accuracy and Authenticity

Is the author well qualified in this field so that the information can be considered reliable?
What is the date of the publication? Is it a reprint?
Are the facts and theories clearly distinguished?
Do the text and illustrations avoid stereotypes?
Do the illustrations contribute to meaningful concepts?
Is anthropomorphism avoided?
Is the book realistic?

Content and Style

Are specific facts given?
Does the author avoid "talking down?"
Are new words explained in the text and illustrations?
Is it readable, with technical language presented at the appropriate level?
Does the book encourage further curiosity?

Illustrations

Do the illustrations clarify and extend the text?
Are captions included to identify and/or explain the illustrations?
Are the illustrations pleasingly spaced?
Are diagrams explained?

Organization

Does the book include a table of contents and index which clearly reflect the content?
Does the book have a pronunciation guide?
Is the information in the book easily located?

Biographies

Are the sources authentic?
Is it a true portrayal of the individual's characteristics and personality?
Are the incidents wisely selected?
Is the individual of interest to children?
Does the book have a place in the curriculum?

Wide Range of Appeal

Will the book be of interest to more than one grade level?
What is the reading level of the book?
Is the book one of special information or generalized knowledge?

RESOURCES

Internet:

Caldecott Medal

http://www.ala.org/alsc/caldecott.html

Sponsored by the American Library Association and the Association for Library Service to Children, the medal is presented annually to the illustrator of the most distinguished American picture book for children published in the United States in the preceding year. The recipient must be a citizen or resident of the United States.

Children's Literature Web Guide

http://www.acs.ucalgary.ca/~dkbrown

This web site has links to lists of the year's best books, children's book awards, bestsellers, authors on the web and more.

Coretta Scott King Award

http://www.ala.org/srrt/csking/index.html

Sponsored by the American Library Association – Social Responsibilities Round Table, this award commemorates the life and work of the late Dr. Martin Luther King, Jr., and honors Mrs. King.

Presented annually to an African American author and an African American illustrator for an inspirational and educational contribution published during the previous year.

Newbery Medal

http://www.ala.org/alsc/nmedal.html

Sponsored by the American Library Association and the Association for Library Service to Children, this medal is presented annually to the author of the most distinguished contribution to American literature for children published in the United States in the preceding year. The recipient must be a citizen or resident of the United States.

Notable Books and Other "Best of" Lists

http://www.ala.org/alsc/awards.html

Association for Library Service to Children – each year a new list of notable resources for children is posted on this web site. Materials covered are books, computer software, videos, web sites, etc.

Books:

Bauer, Caroline Feller, *Caroline Feller Bauer's New Handbook For Storytellers: With Stories, Poems, Magic and More.* Chicago, IL: American Library Association, 1995.

Includes booklists for a variety of activities.

Carter, Betty B., *Best Books for Young Adults, 2nd edition.* Chicago, IL: American Library Association, 2000.

The Young Adult Services Association of ALA created this guide to the ever-changing world of young adult literature.

Children's Books in Print. New Providence, NJ: RR Bowker, annual.

This is a comprehensive list of 188,000 children's titles in print along with lists of children's book award winners, publisher's addresses and phone numbers.

Children's Catalog, 18th edition. Brooklyn, NY: H. W. Wilson Co. 2001.

A comprehensive list of fiction and nonfiction books and magazines for children from preschool through grade six, primarily for the public library collection.

The Elementary School Library Collection: A Guide to Books and Other Media, 22nd edition. Williamsport, PA: Brodart Co., 2000.

A primary source for the development and maintenance of library collections in elementary schools.

Magazines for Kids and Teens, revised edition. Newark, DE: International Reading Association, 1997.

Annotated list of 200 publications with descriptions and ordering information.

Marantz, Sylvia and Kenneth, *Multicultural Picture Books: Art For Understanding Others.* Worthington, OH: Linworth Publishing Co., Vol. 1, 1994 and Vol. 2, 1997

Book reviews of picture books that authentically depict the life and cultures of many other lands.

Middle and Junior High School Catalog, 8th edition. Brooklyn, NY: H. W. Wilson Co. 2000 + annual supplements.

A national standardized list of materials recommended for middle and junior high schools.

Odean, Kathleen, *Great Books for Boys: More than 600 Books for Boys 2-14.* New York: Ballantine Books, 1998.

Books that appeal to boys and that capture the complexity of boys' lives are listed and annotated in groupings by age group, type and subject areas. A section of resources for parents is included.

Odean, Kathleen, *Great Books for Girls: More than 600 Books to Inspire Today's Girls and Tomorrow's Women.* New York: Ballantine Books, 1997.

Books that appeal to girls and show female characters who are "creative, capable, articulate and intelligent" are listed and annotated in groupings by age group, and type. A section of resources for parents is included.

Senior High School Library Catalog, 15th edition. Brooklyn, NY: H. W. Wilson Co. 1997.

This volume is helpful in three areas: Classified Catalog for nonfiction; Author, Title, Subject and Analytical Index; and a Directory of Publishers and Distributors.

Periodicals:

Book Links
www.ala.org/BookLinks
Published by ALA, each issue has several articles linking books and classrooms.

The Book Report
www.linworth.com
Published bimonthly for secondary level librarians. Regular section of reviews for includes fiction, nonfiction, CD-ROM and software, and videos.

Horn Book
http://www.hbook.com/
Six issues published bi-monthly. Includes reviews of children's through young adult books.

Library Talk
www.linworth.com
Published five times per year for elementary level librarians. Includes reviews of books, CD-ROM, online resources, software, and videos.

Reading Teacher
www.reading.org
Published eight times per year by the International Reading Association, each issue has a section on reviews of children's books.

School Library Journal
www.slj.com
Published monthly. Each issue has a section that covers book reviews, Audiovisuals, CD-ROM and software. Occasional feature articles on specific resources.

Science and Children
www.nsta.org/pubs/sc
Published by the National Science Teachers Association nine months of the year. The March issue includes an annual article on "Outstanding Science Trade Books for Children."

Voice of Youth Advocates (VOYA)
www.voya.com
Published bi-monthly, this periodical focuses on young adult literature reviews of fiction, nonfiction, science fiction/fantasy/horror, and CD-ROM.

Young Children
www.naeyc.org
Published six times a year by the National Association for the Education of Young Children. A regular feature is "Children's Books and Videos."

CD-ROM:

Focus on Books (CD-ROM) Updated Edition. Los Angeles, CA: Library Services, Los Angeles Unified School District, 2000.
http://www.lausd.k12.ca.us/lausd/offices/instruct/itb/libserv/
This compilation includes bibliographic information and annotations of 35,000 children's books from Pre-K through grade 12. It can be searched by title, keyword, language, and curricular keyword.

BOOKTALKS

Booktalks are not:
- reviews of books
- book reports
- reading a book out loud

Booktalks are:
- short presentations, 30 seconds to 5 minutes long
- designed to get the audience to read the books presented
- more like storytelling or acting
- commercials for books you like

Booktalk Structure

Many booktalks are structured around three parts:
1. The hook – something that grabs the audience's attention.
2. The content – this gives a flavor of the book, character or plot.
3. The cliffhanger – the booktalk stops, leaving something unresolved and motivating the reader to read the book to find out what happens next.

Think about the previews of coming attractions you see at the movie theater. How do they entice you to pay for a ticket to their upcoming movie?

They start by grabbing your attention; they show you brief scenes, interesting characters you care about and action; and then they leave you wanting to find out more. That is how your booktalk should be structured – leave the students wanting to know more about the book.

How to create a booktalk

1. **Read the book**
   Read lots of books – you cannot effectively talk about a book you haven't read. The students may ask you a question and you won't know the answer if you haven't read the book.

   It's also very hard to "sell" the book if you don't really know what is in it, but very easy to sell it if you read it <u>and</u> liked it!

2. **Take notes**
   If this is a book that you might booktalk, jot down the essential information:
   - author
   - title
   - plot
   - interesting characters, and
   - an incident or two.

   If there's a quote or description that grabbed your attention, note the page number it appears on. Later on, when you are preparing a booktalk, these notes will be a valuable way to find the exact books to include.

3. **Decide what you want to share**
   Think about your audience and their interests. You might structure your booktalk around one of the following:

   - A scene – one with action, interesting detail and emotion.

   - A character – a person that others would want to know more about.

- The plot – give a summary of the plot up to a point.

4. Write down your booktalk

Writing it down will help you to focus on what to include and give you a chance to revise and edit it to have more impact.

5. Practice

Very few of us are accomplished public speakers. This is a skill that comes from practice.

Read the talk to yourself, out loud, using the same emotion and skill that you will use with the students. Use movement, facial expression, voice and drama to bring the talk to life.

Practice it in front of your cat, your own children, or the plants in your living room. You might tape record it or video tape yourself to see how you sound and look while giving it.

The goal is to get to a point where you know the talk and don't have to rely on reading it or on your notes to remember where you are.

6. Try it out

Give the talk and evaluate how it went. You may want to make some changes because it was too long or you forgot a key point. Students may have responded to something that you didn't feel was very important causing you to beef up that part of your talk and cut something else out.

As students and interests change over the years, or from class to class, you may need to change aspects of your talk.

7. File your notes and script for future reference

You may give this talk again in the future and having your notes and script will refresh your memory and save you from having to create a new talk all over again from scratch.

Remember – booktalks are designed to get books read, so be sure to have copies of the books on hand. It will frustrate students if you talk about books that are already checked out or otherwise not available. An excellent way to increase booktalking is to teach students to do it for their favorite books.

RESOURCES

Books:

Littlejohn, Carol, *Keep Talking That Book: Booktalks to Promote Reading, Vol. 2.* Worthington, OH: Linworth Publishing, Inc., 2000.

Littlejohn, Carol, *Keep Talking That Book: Booktalks to Promote Reading, Vol. 3.* Worthington, OH: Linworth Publishing, Inc., 2001.

Littlejohn, Carol, *Talk That Book: Booktalks to Promote Reading.* Worthington, OH: Linworth Publishing, Inc., 1999.

Polette, Nancy, *Multi-Cultural Readers' Theatre: Booktalks.* O'Fallon, MO: Booklures, 1994.

STORYTELLING

Before humans learned to write, knowledge was passed from generation to generation by storytelling. The people who kept this vast history in their memories and passed it on were revered for their knowledge and their abilities. But even though the stories had a specific purpose, they were also loved because they were entertaining.

Today we pass on our history through written records and computerized databases, and yet the storyteller has an important role to play. Many modern storytellers use music, film and video to tell their stories, but there is something very special about live storytelling. It is a participatory experience that is shared by the audience and the storyteller. The audience reacts to the storyteller and the storyteller reacts to the audience. No matter how many times a storyteller tells the same story, each time it will be a different experience because the audience is different.

It is live theater.

Finding your stories

Stories are all around us, in our daily lives and in our memories. The best places to find stories are in books – read, read! Look at collections of stories, fairy tales, and poetry as well as novels and picture books.

When you find a story, make notes about it – a sentence or two on the plot, the author, title of the story, and, if it is in a collection, the name of the collection. These notes will help you to find that story when you need it.

Look for stories that have:

A simple, clear plot – Complicated plot lines are difficult to tell as a story. Also, keeping the plot in one sequence helps the audience to understand what's happening easier than with flashbacks or parallel story lines.

A few clearly defined characters – It's hard for a listener to keep track of many characters or characters that are very similar.

Fast-paced action – Long descriptions or thoughtful passages may <u>read</u> well, but action <u>tells</u> well.

A good sound – Read the story aloud to hear how it sounds. Writing for someone to speak the words is different than writing for someone to read the words. Can the story be rewritten so it will sound good?

Steps to storytelling

1. **Audience**
   Consider who will be in your audience, the size of your audience, the purpose of the story, and where you will be telling the story. All of these factors will influence what story you decide to tell and how you will tell it.

2. **Select the story**
   Is the purpose to entertain? Do you have a theme or subject in mind? Have you been asked to tell a specific type of story? See the criteria listed at the start of this section to select a story.

3. Plan the story

Think about what you will include in your story: characters, actions, words or phrases of dialog, and descriptions.

As you plan the story, visualize it – see the setting, the characters and the action as it takes place in your imagination. You might prepare a storyboard of the sequence of the story or draw it as a story map or flow chart.

Eliminate unnecessary characters and actions to streamline the story.

Plan an engaging beginning – something to "hook" the audience and bring them into the story.

4. Read the story aloud

Listen to how it sounds. Does it have flow and rhythm? Is there a beginning, middle and end? Is it too long or too short?

Have someone listen to you read it. Ask them if it held their attention and what they thought of it.

5. Practice telling it

Learn the story by practicing it over and over again. If possible, learn it so well you won't need to use notes and so the story comes naturally to you.

Remember that storytelling is a dramatic art and be sure to use your voice, gesture, and body movements to convey the action and the emotion of the story.

Use a camcorder to video tape yourself so you can hear and see what the audience would see.

Don't try to memorize the story word for word. Visualize it, don't memorize it. See the story in your imagination as you are telling it and let the images guide you in your telling.

6. Perform your story

Some things to consider when performing:

- Warm-up – plan a way to get the audience's attention and prepare them for the story. You might introduce yourself and the theme or background for the story (or stories) you are about to tell. Some storytellers use a bell or light the storyteller's candle to signal the start of the story time.

- Stage – most often you will not have a stage setting, so consider where you will stand in the room. Is the background too cluttered or will it be distracting to the audience?

- Sight and sound – can everyone in the audience see you? Will the audience be seated? Do you need to be on a raised platform? Remember to keep eye contact with members of the audience. Can everyone hear you? Are there background noises that may be distracting? Do you need to use a microphone?

- Props/costume – do you need to use props or some type of costume to better relate the story? For example, a change of hats could be used to show a change in characters. Props can help you remember key points in the story and also help the audience focus.

Remember to have fun!

RESOURCES

Books:

Bauer, Caroline Feller, *Caroline Feller Bauer's New Handbook for Storytellers: With Stories, Poems, Magic and More.* Chicago, IL: American Library Association, 1995.

Holt, David and Bill Mooney, editors, *Ready-to-Tell-Tales: Sure-Fire Stories from America's Favorite Storytellers.* Little Rock, AR: August House Publishers, 1994.

MacDonald, Margaret Read, *Bookplay: 101 Creative Themes to Share with Young Children.* Northahven, CT: Library Professional Publication (an imprint of Shoe String Press), 1995.

Marsh, Valerie, *The Storyteller's Sampler.* Fort Atkinson, WI: Alleyside Press (an imprint of Highsmith Press), 1996,

Mooney, Bill and David Holt, editors, *The Storyteller's Guide: Storytellers Share Advice for the Classroom, Boardroom, Showroom, Podium, Pulpit and Center Stage.* Little Rock, AR: August House Publishers, 1996.

INFORMATION SKILLS

"Knowledge is knowing – or knowing where to find out."
Alvin Toffler

Skills needed to effectively use a library and access information can be divided into three major categories:

Library Orientation – how to use one specific library;
Information Skills – how to find and use information and resources in a library;
Information Literacy – includes a broader set of skills needed to access, evaluate and use information effectively, in a variety of settings.

This section will provide an overview of some skills that might be included in a program of library instruction, some ideas for activities and lessons, and a list of additional resources that can be useful in building your library instruction program.

Research has shown that people learn better when the learning is relevant, that is, when it relates to something in their lives and builds upon their past experience and knowledge. Learning also occurs best when there is immediate hands-on practice of the skills. This also applies to library and information skills.

Students learn information skills best when:

- they are relevant to what the student is learning in class or to the student's interests;
- they fill an immediate need of the student's;
- the student can practice the skills immediately after learning them.

Prepackaged programs of library skills are not as effective as those tailored to meet the needs of your students and that reflect the library program at your school.

Before a class visits the library, talk to the teacher about what is happening in the classroom. Does the teacher want the students to find materials about a specific topic? Are certain skills being emphasized? How can the library's resources and specific information skills support what is happening in the classroom?

Your school may have implemented an information literacy curriculum and specific skills may be integrated with what happens in the classroom. Find out if there is such a curriculum and how you fit into it.

However, if you have no experience teaching library and information skills and your school has no curriculum in place, there are many commercially prepared skills activities and books with ideas that you can adapt.

Library Orientation Skills

A library is a very specialized place that is difficult to understand without some instruction. Materials are arranged on shelves with strange numbers or letters on them. Libraries also have specialized rules that need to be understood.

Even when presenting library orientation skills, be sure to connect what students are learning in the library to what they learn in the classroom. For example, the difference between fiction and nonfiction can relate to their language arts and science lessons.

The first skills students learn are often library orientation skills, including:

1. How your library is organized:
   - Give a tour of the library – show where things are located;
   - Fiction/nonfiction- differences;
   - Dewey Decimal system;
   - Location of special collections.

2. Library policies and rules:
   - Care of books and materials;
   - Rules for behavior and consequences.

3. How to check out materials:
   - Procedures for check out, such as use of shelf markers, etc.;
   - Time period for checkouts;
   - Overdues and fines.

Information Skills

Once a student understands how your library is organized they need to know more specific skills to be able to locate the materials and resources they need and then how to use what they have found. Traditional library skills were based on knowing how to use print resources effectively and, though those skills are still useful and necessary, students must also master the skills needed to use electronic and online resources.

Information skills include:
   1. Parts of a book/resource:
      - Author, title, call number, and so forth

2. Types of materials and how they are organized:
   - Fiction/nonfiction;
   - Dewey Decimal Classification System.

3. How to find materials in the library:
   - Use of the catalog (card or online);
   - How to search by author, title, keyword, subject;
   - Databases (print, such as Reader's Guide, or online).

4. How to find materials online:
   - Online searching skills.

5. How to use specific resources and collections in the library:
   - Printed materials – almanac, atlas, dictionary, encyclopedia, and other specialized resources;
   - Bibliographic information, guide words, indexes, table of contents;
   - Formats of specific materials (i.e. Readers' Guide citation);
   - Databases – online searching skills specific to each resource.

Information Literacy Skills

Information literacy extends beyond specific information skills to a broader set of skills that enable a person to:
   - access,
   - evaluate, and
   - use information effectively.

A set of nine information literacy standards has been developed as part of *Information Power: Building Partnerships for Learning*, the national school library guidelines. See the standards on page 94 and *Information Power* for more details, including indicators of student achievement and descriptions of the levels of proficiency for each indicator.

Information literacy skills are most often used when students are conducting research for a specific class assignment, but the skills also have application in many real life settings.

There are several models for information literacy and research skills. Two popular models are the Big6™ and FLIP it!™ which are briefly described below.

The Big6™
by Michael Eisenberg and Robert Berkowitz

This wellknown and widely used model focuses on six steps, which form the basis for a series of tasks and skills.

Step 1 – Task Definition
What needs to be done?
- Define the problem
- Identify the information needed

Step 2 – Information Seeking Strategies
What resources can I use?
- Determine all possible sources
- Select the best sources

Step 3 – Location and Access
Where can I find these resources?
- Locate sources
- Find information within sources

Step 4 – Use of Information
What can I use from these resources?
- Engage (e.g., read, hear, view)
- Extract relevant information

Step 5 – Synthesis
What can I make to finish the job?
- Organize information from multiple sources
- Present the result

Step 6 – Evaluation
How will I know I did my job well?
- Judge the result (effectiveness)
- Judge the process (efficiency)

Big6 Skills, Copyright 1987, Eisenberg and Berkowitz. Reprinted with permission. For more information see www. big6.com.

FLIP it!™
by Alice Yucht

FLIP it!™ is a generic strategy based on the question, "If? … Then." The letters stand for:

F Focus – specifying
- What do I really need to do and/or find out?
- What are the crucial questions I need to answer?

L Links – strategizing
- What connections can I use to get the information I need?
- What's the best/most logical way to accomplish my goals?

I Input – sorting, storing, sifting
- What kinds of information do I need to find/use?
- What's the most useful way to organize and apply what I know?

P Payoff – solving, showing
- How can I best demonstrate what I've learned?
- What is now the best solution to my original problem?

it Intelligent Thinking or If/Then
- Did I use my brains effectively? Use as an evaluation checkpoint to keep on track by asking, "If I know… then I should…"

FLIPit reprinted with permission.

The Nine Information Literacy Standards for Student Learning

Information Literacy

The student who is information literate…

Standard 1: accesses information efficiently and effectively.

Standard 2: evaluates information critically and competently.

Standard 3: uses information accurately and creatively.

Independent Learning

The student who is an independent learner is information literate and…

Standard 4: pursues information related to personal interests.

Standard 5: appreciates literature and other creative expressions of information.

Standard 6: strives for excellence in information seeking and knowledge generation.

Social Responsibility

The student who contributes positively to the learning community and to society is information literate and…

Standard 7: recognizes the importance of information to a democratic society.

Standard 8: practices ethical behavior in regard to information and information technology.

Standard 9: participates effectively in groups to pursue and generate information.

From *Information Power: Building Partnerships for Learning* by American Library Association and Association for Educational Communications and Technology. Copyright ©1998 American Library Association and Association for Educational Communications and Technology. Reprinted with permission of the American Library Association.

RESOURCES

INTERNET:

FLIP it!™
http://www.aliceinfo.org/
Alice Yucht's web site has extensive information on FLIP it!™, her information skills strategy.

BIG6™
www.big6.com/
The BIG6™ web site has additional information on the use of the BIG6™ as well as sample lessons that incorporate the BIG6™.

BOOKS:

Allen, Christine, editor, *Skills for Life: Information Literacy for Grades K-6, 2nd edition.* Worthington, OH: Linworth Publishing, Inc., 1999.

Allen, Christine and Mary Alice Anderson, editors., *Skills for Life: Information Literacy for Grades 7-12, 2nd edition.* Worthington, OH: Linworth Publishing, Inc., 1999.

Anderson, Mary Alice, editor, *Teaching Information Literacy Using Electronic Resources for Grades 6-12.* Worthington, OH: Linworth Publishing, Inc., 1996.

California Media and Library Educators Association, *From Library Skills to Information Literacy: A Handbook for the 21st Century; 2nd edition.* San Jose, CA: Hi Willow Research and Publishing, 1997.

Eisenberg, Michael and Robert Berkowitz, *The BIG6™ Collection: The Best of the BIG6™ Newsletter.* Worthington, OH: Linworth Publishing, Inc., 2000.

Eisenberg, Michael and Robert Berkowitz, *The New, Improved BIG6™ Workshop Handbook.* Worthington, OH: Linworth Publishing, Inc., 1999.

Eisenberg, Michael and Robert Berkowitz, with Barbara Jansen and Tami Little, *Teaching Information & Technology Skills: The BIG6™ in Elementary Schools.* Worthington, OH: Linworth Publishing, Inc., 1999.

Eisenberg, Michael and Robert Berkowitz with Robert Darrow and Kathleen L. Spitzer, *Teaching Information and Technology Skills: The Big6™ in Secondary Schools.* Worthington, OH: Linworth Publishing, Inc., 2000.

Farmer, Lesley S.J., *Cooperative Activities in the Library Media Center, 2nd edition.* Englewood, CO: Libraries Unlimited, Inc., 1999.

Kasowitz, Abby S., *Using the Big6™ to Teach and Learn With the Internet.* Worthington, OH: Linworth Publishing, Inc., 2000.

Skeele, Linda, editor, *Teaching Information Literacy Using Electronic Resources for Grades K-6.* Worthington, OH: Linworth Publishing, Inc., 1996.

Yucht, Alice H., *FLIP IT!™ An Information Skills Strategy for Student Researchers.* Worthington, OH: Linworth Publishing, Inc., 1997.

OTHER RESOURCES:

Essential Skills for the Information Age: The Big6™ in Action (video). Worthington, OH: Linworth Publishing, Inc., ©1999.
www.linworth.com
Featuring Michael Eisenberg in action with groups of students of varying ages, this video provides information on what the Big6™ approach is and how it works.

Know It All Video Series. Lincoln, NE: GPN.
http://gpn.unl.edu
This series of 15-minute videos, developed in collaboration with the American Association of School Librarians, teaches the skills of information literacy in nine classroom videos designed for grades 3-6. Four professional development videos are also included. Video #13, *Information Literacy Standards for Student Learning,* is an overview of the national standards given in *Information Power.*

Super Sleuth. Richmond, VA: RTC.
http://www.calendarclue.com/
This is a detective-type game used to teach basic reference skills in school library/media centers, (for grades 3-5).

SAMPLE INFORMATION SKILLS ACTIVITIES

Dewey Activities

- **Book talk the Dewey sections**
  Pick a few books from one Dewey section to highlight the variety of subjects in that section. Be sure to alternate sections with different classes during the week or students will quickly deplete the section you are highlighting.

- **How to organize books**
  Place a few books on each table with their call numbers covered. Ask students how many ways they could organize the books and have them record their answers. Then ask them to think of the best way – usually they will come up with subject. That can lead into how the Dewey Decimal System organizes information by subject.

- **Dewey crafts**
  Have groups of students design posters for each Dewey section, illustrating them with photos from magazines or original artwork. Hang the posters from the ceiling by the shelves with those numbers. Students could also design quilt squares (out of paper) that could be put together with a backing and hung in the library.

- **Dewey Bingo**
  Have students divide a piece of paper into nine parts and write their choice of nine Dewey sections in each part. Show a book with call number covered and ask them to think of the Dewey number for that type of book and mark their bingo card.

- **Dewey order**
  Write several call numbers each on one sheet of card stock. Give each card to a student who pretends to be a book with that call number. The students must arrange themselves in order by call number without speaking. Ask the class if they did it correctly. Then have each student go to the place on the shelf where they would be if they were the book.

Library Orientation
(see also Library Rules on page 19)

- **Read a book**
  There are a number of children's books about libraries that can be used to begin library orientation or to humorously explore libraries. Here are a few titles to consider:

  Deedy, Carmen, *The Library Dragon*. Atlanta, GA: Peachtree Pub., 1994.

  Ernst, Lisa Campbell, *Stella Louella's Runaway Book*. New York: Simon & Schuster Books for Young Readers, 1998.

  Kimmel, Eric A., *I Took My Frog to the Library*. New York: Puffin Books, 1990.

  Miller, William, *Richard Wright and the Library Card*. New York: Lee & Low Books, 1997.

  Stewart, Sarah, *The Library*. New York: Farrar Straus Giroux, 1995.

  Thaler, Mike, *Librarian from the Black Lagoon*. New York: Scholastic, 1997.

- **Map of Library**
  Create a large bulletin board map of the library. As you describe where things are located, put labels on the bulletin board.

  For a review at a later time remove the labels from the bulletin board. Give students their own map of the library and a list of things in the library, such as encyclopedias, online catalog, fiction books, or magazines. Ask them to work in pairs to find out where everything is located and write it on their map. Bring the whole class together and have them label the large bulletin board map.

- **Library Treasure Hunt**
  Give clues to a library "treasure" and ask teams of students to identify and locate it. For example, the "treasure" might be a CD-ROM atlas. Clues could include: I have maps of all kinds; I help people learn about the earth; I can be searched; You can print my pages.

Information Skills

Remember that information skills are best taught in context, when they meet an immediate need and when students have time to practice them.

- **Parts of a book**
  Even if your library catalog is online, it's important for students to know what an author, title, and subject heading are. As they continue in school and develop research reports, they will need to know how to cite a work.

  Read a book to the class. Then ask the class the following questions:

  Who wrote the words for this book?
  Author

Who drew the pictures?
Illustrator
What is this book called?
Title
What is the book about?
Subject

Write the answers to their questions on a large sheet of paper in catalog card format. Explain to the students what the parts are called.

- **Catalog card**
  Give each student a book and a sheet of paper with blanks where the information would appear on a catalog card. Ask each student to put the correct information for their book on the paper.

- **Find the book**
  Give each student a catalog card and ask them to find the book on the shelf.

- **Find the answer**
  Student teams are given a set of questions on index cards and must find the answer in the library's resources and write down where they found it.

DEWEY DECIMAL CLASSIFICATION SYSTEM

The Dewey Decimal Classification System was designed by Melvil Dewey in 1873 as a way to organize knowledge. Each of the major sections covers a broad topic and is divided into smaller sections of more specialized topics (see list on page 101). The Dewey Decimal system is used worldwide, in more that 135 countries, and in almost all school and public libraries in the United States.

The Dewey Decimal system is a classification system. This means that the number assigned to a work represents the subject matter content of the work and items with similar content are grouped together within the same number. Using a classification system allows for browsing the shelves, because books on the same topic will be next to each other.

Each book is given a call number. Call numbers are those letters, numbers and symbols (used separately or in combination) that are assigned to a book to show its location in the library shelving system.

The major categories within the Dewey Decimal System are:

001-099	General Knowledge
100-199	Philosophy and Psychology
200-299	Religion
300-399	Social Sciences
400-499	Language
500-599	Natural Sciences
600-699	Applied Sciences
700-799	Arts and Recreation
800-899	Drama and Poetry
900-999	Travel, Biography, and History

Within these major categories are further divisions that represent narrower topics. A regular number followed by a decimal point and several numbers after the decimal point is very narrowly defined.

Example:

```
973.7
Bla    Black, Wallace B.
           Slaves to Soldiers: African-
       American Fighting Men in the
       Civil War.
```

The broader number "970" represents the General History of North America; "973" narrows it down to the History of the United States; "973.7" is the Civil War.

The numbers after the period are treated as decimals, therefore 973.65 would come before 973.7. It helps to think of it as money - .65 (65 cents) comes before .7 (70 cents).

The letters on the line below the number refer to the author's last name. This keeps the books on the Civil War in alphabetical order by author

For more detailed information and resources on the Dewey Decimal System see the Resources listed on page 100.

RESOURCES

Internet:

Dewey Decimal Classification System – this web site includes DDC summaries, a brief introduction, a bibliography and a free screensaver that you can download in addition to other links and online resources.
www.oclc.org/fp

"Do We Really Know Dewey?" – teaches about the Dewey Decimal System. This site was created by the Nettleton Intermediate Center, Jonesboro, Arkansas.
http://tqjunior.advanced.org/5002/

Books:

Abridged Dewey Decimal Classification and Relative Index, 13th edition. Dublin, OH: OCLC Forest Press, 1997.

Davis, Sydney W. and Gregory R. New, *Abridged 13 Workbook.* Dublin, OH: OCLC Forest Press, 1997.

Other:

Dewey Bookmarks (available in English and Spanish). Dublin, OH: OCLC Forest Press.

"Dot Marks the Spot" Dewey Poster for Children (available in English and Spanish). Dublin, OH: OCLC Forest Press, 2000.

Dewey Decimal System Kit, includes 15 copies of a paperback book on the Dewey Decimal Classification System, 16 posters, blackline masters and 200 bookmarks. Cleveland, OH: World Almanac Education.
http://worldalmanac.com/kits.asp

DEWEY DECIMAL CLASSIFICATION SYSTEM

000 Generalities
010 Bibliography
020 Library and information sciences
030 General encyclopedic works
050 General serial publications
060 General organizations and museology
070 News media, journalism, publishing
080 General collections
090 Manuscripts and rare books

100 Philosophy and Psychology
110 Metaphysics
120 Epistemology, causation, humankind
130 Paranormal phenomena
140 Specific philosophical schools
150 Psychology
160 Logic
170 Ethics (Moral philosophy)
180 Ancient, medieval, Oriental philosophy
190 Modern western philosophy

200 Religion
210 Philosophy and theory of religion
220 Bible
230 Christianity, Christian theology
240 Christian moral and devotional theology
250 Christian orders and local church
260 Social and ecclesiastical theology
270 History of Christianity and Christian church
280 Christian denominations and sects
290 Comparative religion and other religions

300 Social Sciences
310 Collections of general statistics
320 Political science
330 Economics
340 Law
350 Public administration and military science
360 Social problems and services; association
370 Education
380 Commerce, communications, transportation
390 Customs, etiquette, folklore

400 Language
410 Linguistics
420 English and Old English
430 Germanic languages, German
440 Romance languages, French
450 Italian, Romanian, Rhaeto-Romanic
460 Spanish and Portuguese languages
470 Italic languages, Latin
480 Hellenic languages, Classical Greek
490 Other languages

500 Natural Sciences and Mathematics
510 Mathematics
520 Astronomy and allied sciences
530 Physics
540 Chemistry and allied sciences
550 Earth sciences
560 Paleontology, paleozoology
570 Life sciences, biology
580 Plants
590 Animals

600 Technology (Applied Sciences)
610 Medical sciences, Medicine
620 Engineering and allied operations
630 Agriculture and related technologies
640 Home economics and family living
650 Management and auxiliary services
660 Chemical engineering
670 Manufacturing
680 Manufacture for specific uses
690 Buildings

700 The Arts, Fine and Decorative Arts
710 Civic and landscape art
720 Architecture
730 Plastic arts, sculpture
740 Drawing and decorative arts
750 Painting and paintings
760 Graphic arts, printmaking and prints
770 Photography and photographs
780 Music
790 Recreational and performing arts

800 Literature and Rhetoric
810 American literature in English
820 English and Old English literatures
830 Literatures of Germanic languages
840 Literatures of Romance languages
850 Italian, Romanian, Rhaeto-Romanic
860 Spanish and Portuguese literatures
870 Italic literatures, Latin
880 Hellenic literatures, Classical Greek
890 Literatures of other languages

900 Geography and History
910 Geography and travel
920 Biography, genealogy, insignia
930 History of ancient world to ca. 499
940 General history of Europe
950 General history of Asia, Far East
960 General history of Africa
970 General history of North America
980 General history of South America
990 General history of other areas

THE INTERNET

The Internet is a global network of computers that is interconnected via modems, phone lines, cables, satellites and servers. The Internet is also known as "The Net," or "The Information Super Highway." The Internet makes it possible to share files, post information and receive messages. This section will provide a brief overview of the Internet and some of the issues facing school libraries. Reading about the Internet is no substitute for actually getting hands-on training and experience using it.

Internet Services

The Internet provides a vast array of tools and resources for educators. There are many types of files that can be retrieved including software, text, sound, graphics, images and video. These files include lesson plans, reference works, maps, student published information and online library catalogs. Individuals can set up email accounts, do research, subscribe to a listserv, chat with others, shop, and take classes or workshops online.

A common analogy of the Internet is that it is like a highway. A highway has many lanes to travel and many options such as on-ramps, exits, scenic routes and other connecting roads where people can travel at different speeds and for different purposes.

One difference is that highways and roads have some controlling authority that regulates the traffic, determines where the roads will go, how they will be maintained, and provides a structure and regulations for their use. The Internet, while it has some accepted ways of doing business, is more like the Wild West with people creating their own roads, their own on and off ramps and often charging for the privilege of using their road.

The Web

The World Wide Web (WWW) is the most popular lane on the Internet highway. It uses a Graphical User Interface (GUI), which allows for text, graphics and "hot" links. These links allow users to jump or surf from one site to another. In this way it departs from the idea of a highway. On the Web you can leap from one spot on the highway to another spot in another country almost instantaneously.

Web Addresses

Each web page has an address, called an URL (Universal Resource Locator). These addresses begin with "http://" and usually include "www." The URL allows anyone connected to the Web to leap to that web page.

Domain names indicate the person or organization that is hosting the web site. For example, the Library of Congress domain name is "loc.gov." The last part of the domain name is a clue to the type of entity. Some others are:

- .com commercial;
- .org organization, usually nonprofit;
- .edu college or university;
- .gov government agency;
- .net companies or organizations with large networks.

For example, http://www.dpi.state.wi.us, is the domain name for the Department of Public Instruction (DPI) for Wisconsin and it tells you it is part of a state, the name of the state (wi) and that it is in the United States (us).

However, it is not always easy to find out who has created a specific web site. There are no bibliographic controls such as MARC records for the web.

Email addresses have a name (sometimes just a combination of letters and numbers) followed by "@" and the domain name. The email address for the President is president@whitehouse.gov.

Viewing and Searching the Web

To view web sites you will need a browser. The two most popular are Netscape Communicator and Microsoft Internet Explorer.

With the millions upon millions of web sites now available on the web, it would be impossible to know the address for each one, or to find and catalog them by yourself. There are online services called search engines that scan the Internet using key words and phrases that the customer enters and return a list of the web sites that best match the request. These search engines are constantly scouring the Internet for new sites and adding new information to their index.

Some of these search engines have Directories – their staff locate sites and create data bases, classifying the sites to provide convenient access to resources. Yahoo!® for example, provides categories such as "Recreation & Sports," "Business & Economy," and "Education."

There are many search engines and each works slightly differently. Try them out and find one that fits your needs.

Search engines, like so many of the sites on the Web, are commercial enterprises and advertisements appear regularly on the computer screen.

Some popular search engines are:

AltaVista
http://www.altavista.com

Excite
http://www.excite.com

Google
http://www.google.com

Hotbot
http://www.hotbot.com

Lycos
http://www.lycos.com

Yahoo!
http://yahoo.com

Meta-search engines send your query to many search engines at the same time. Some even allow you to specify which search engines to use in the search or you can leave it to the meta-searcher to choose the best three or the fastest three engines.

Meta-search engines are useful if you are looking for a unique term or phrase (enclose phrases in quotes); or if you simply want to test run a couple of keywords to see if they get what you want. For more complex searches that use Boolean operators, it's probably best to run the search in a single search engine.

As anyone who does Internet searching knows, search protocol (the way you enter search keywords) is far from standardized and this means that meta-search engines may not always be successful in translating the Boolean symbols used for each engine.

Some of the better meta-search engines are:

> www.profusion.com
> www.37.com
> www.metacrawler.com (Power Search)

Internet Filters

Now that most school libraries are connected to the Internet, we face a difficult question: Should we provide unrestricted access to the Internet or should we install filtering software? Either choice comes with its own set of issues and problems.

In December 2000, the President signed a new law that places restrictions on the use of certain categories of federal funding. The restrictions require Internet safety policies and the use of technology which blocks certain material from being accessed through the Internet from school sites, including school libraries. Your state may also have laws relating to Internet filtering.

WHAT YOU CAN DO

Check your school and district policies related to Internet access and filtering to determine what you should be doing in your library.

If your library will be installing filtering software, here are some questions to ask and some things to consider.

How does filtering software work?

Two types of Internet filters are available. Users can either purchase a product that installs on the network server, or subscribe to a service offered by their Internet Service Provider (ISP). Typically, both local and remote server versions operate via a "proxy" server that does not allow individual workstations to connect directly to the Internet. This way when a user attempts to access restricted web pages, the proxy server intercepts the browser's request and may deny it based on user-configured criteria.

Filtering or blocking software restricts access to Internet content through a variety of means. It may scan a web site's content based on keywords, phrases or strings of text. It may also restrict access based on the source of the information or through a ratings system assigned by a third party (based on sexual content, violence, nudity, and so forth).

What are some points to consider when using Internet filters?

Whether your library uses an Internet filtering program or not, there is still no substitute for having an acceptable use policy in place and teaching students to use good judgment when searching the Internet. Filters can be used effectively in schools, but they can also give a false sense of security. With or without filters, some students will still try, and succeed, in finding objectionable sites.

Before selecting an Internet filter, do some research on how each product works.

Here are some key points to consider:

1. The stoplist must be reasonably accurate and effective at blocking pornography.

2. The stoplist must be customizable so as to block only pornographic content.

3. It must be possible for the library to add and delete sites from the stoplist.

4. It must be possible for the librarian to override the filter for the patron.

5. It must be possible for all keyword blocking to be turned off.

6. The vendor has demonstrated it will quickly unblock incorrectly blocked sites.

7. The vendor has demonstrated that it is a responsible member of the software industry by only making accurate claims about their product and by conducting its public relations in a responsible manner.

Internet Filtering Products

Here are some companies and products that filter the Internet.
Note: All products listed below offer free trials.

Bess
N2H2, Inc.
(800) 971-2622
www.n2h2.com

CyberPatrol and Surf Control
Surf Control, Inc.
(800) 368-3366
www.surfcontrol.com

WatchGuard
WatchGuard Technologies
(800) 734-9905
www.watchguard.com

WebSense
Websense, Inc.
(800) 723-1166
www.websense.com

X-Stop
8e6 Technologies
(888) 786-7999
www.8e6technologies.com

INTERNET RESOURCES

Searching the Internet:

Choose the Best Search Engine for Your Information Needs
www.nueva.pvt.k12.ca.us/~debbie/library/research/adviceengine.html

Internet Search Engine Guide
www.searchengineguide.com/

Recommended Search Strategy
www.lib.berkeley.edu/TeachingLib/Guides/Internet/Strategies.html

Internet Filtering:

American Civil Liberties Union – Cyber-Liberties Page
www.aclu.org/issues/cyber/hmcl.html

American Library Association – Office for Intellectual Freedom
www.ala.org/oif.html

American Library Association – Children's Internet Protection Act Web Site
www.ala.org/cipa

American Library Association – Libraries & the Internet Toolkit
www.ala.org/alaorg/oif/internettoolkit.html

CyberAngels
www.cyberangels.org

General Library Internet Resources:

Library Journal Buyer's Guide
www.ljdigital.com/buyersguide/
  With more than 500 companies and 400 product and service categories, this site is the one-stop online catalog for librarians. This is the web-based version of the long-popular print supplement to *Library Journal* and *School Library Journal*.

Library Land
http://sunsite.berkeley.edu/LibraryLand/
  An excellent starting point for links to library-related web pages. Areas covered include administration, audiovisual, automation, children's services, electronic resources, Internet librarianship, reader's advisory, reference, and technical services.

Library Media Specialists Academic Village
www.pld.fayette.k12.ky.us/lms/default.htm
  Designed for school library staff in Kentucky, this Virtual Resource Center focuses on providing information supporting LMS activities, such as copyright issues, library administration, electronic journals, curriculum development, online discussion, listservs, and using the web.

LION: Librarians Information Online Network
www.libertynet.org/lion/
  Created as an online resource for K-12 school librarians in Philadelphia and throughout the nation, LION's goals are to offer a comprehensive collection of Internet-based resources of interest to school librarians.

LM_NET On The Web
http://ericir.syr.edu/lm_net/
  LM_NET is a discussion group open to school library media specialists worldwide, and to people involved with the school library media field. It is used by library media people for many different things–to ask for input, share ideas and information, link programs that are geographically remote, make contacts, etc. Visit this web site to subscribe to the listserv or to access discussion topics from the past.

Peter Milbury's School Librarian Web Pages
www.school-libraries.net
  This site is a collection of web pages created or maintained by school librarians. Includes web pages for entire schools, individual school libraries, personal, professional associations, or other curriculum related resources. Also included are a few links helpful to Web development.

Peter Milbury's Online Resources for School Librarians Web Pages
www.school-libraries.org
  A collection of links to numerous resources for school librarians.

School Libraries on the Web: A Directory
http://www.sldirectory.com/
  This is a list of library web pages maintained by K-12 school libraries in the United States and in countries around the world. This Directory is maintained by Linda Bertland.

School Library Journal Online
www.slj.com
  Included are articles from *School Library Journal*; a searchable index; lists of best books, and other resources; book and audiovisual reviews; news from the world of libraries; and many other links.

Professional Organizations on the Internet:

American Association of School Librarians
www.ala.org/aasl/

American Library Association
www.ala.org/

Association for Library Service to
Children
http://ala8.ala.org/alsc/

Children's Book Council
www.cbcbooks.org/

Council on Library/Media Technicians
http://library.ucr.edu/COLT

International Association of School
Librarianship
www.iasl-slo.org/

International, National and State Library
Associations
www.libertynet.org/lion/organizations.html

International Reading Association
www.reading.org/

Young Adult Library Services Association
www.ala.org/yalsa/

Books:

Alexander, Janet E. and Marsha Ann Tate,
*Web Wisdom: How to Evaluate and Create
Information Quality on the Web.* Mahwah,
NJ: Lawrence Erlbaum and Associates,
1999.

Harnack, Andrew and Eugene Kleppinger,
*Online! A Reference Guide to Using
Internet Sources.* New York: St. Martin's
Press, 1997.

Lazarus, Wendy and Laurie Lipper, *The
Parent's Guide to the Information
Superhighway: Rules and Tools for
Families Online.* Washington, DC: The
Children's Partnership, 1998.

Minkel, Walter and Roxanne Hsu Feldman,
*Delivering Web Reference Services to
Young People.* Chicago, IL: American
Library Association, 1999.

Pappas, Margorie, et al, *Searching
Electronic Resources, 2nd edition.*
Worthington, OH: Linworth Publishing, 1998.

Schneider, Karen G., *A Practical Guide to
Internet Filters.* New York: Neal Schuman
Publishers, 1997.

Simpson, Carol and Sharon L. McElmeel,
Internet for Schools: A Practical Guide.
Worthington, OH: Linworth Publishing, 2000.

Online Searching

Different skills are involved in searching online because of the computer's ability to search for specific words or phrases in many combinations and to do it very fast. Searching electronically, whether you are using an Internet search engine, an online library catalog or searching a CD-ROM encyclopedia, almost always uses Boolean logic. This is simply a way of combining words and phrases in a logical manner to locate the information you need.

Concepts

The first step is to determine the major concepts that represent your search. If you want to find out about women who are working in mathematics, two major concepts are "mathematics" and "women."

The second step is to think about how these concepts relate to each other and then to apply search strategies to locate the information you need.

Boolean Logic

AND – Using the word "AND" will search for information that has **both** terms. The search "mathematics AND women" will locate only those records that include **both** the term "mathematics" **and** the term "women," the intersection of the two circles below:

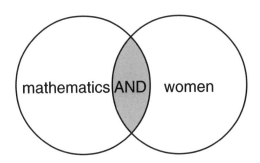

Only if the information contains both words will it be found by your search.

OR – Using the word "OR" will search for information that has **either** term. The search "mathematics OR women" will locate everything on both "mathematics" and everything on "women," that includes everything in both circles:

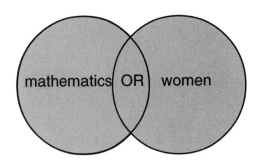

NOT – You can eliminate something from your search by using the term NOT. The search "mathematics NOT women" will locate everything with the word "mathematics" and eliminate those that also have the word "women." Use this command carefully as it may eliminate records that are valuable to your search. This term will locate everything in the mathematics circle minus the intersection.

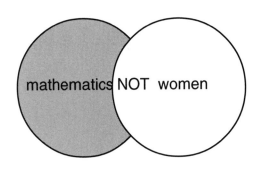

Wildcard Characters

Most electronic search systems will allow for a wildcard character to replace a letter or to allow you to truncate a word. Different characters are used as wildcard characters in different programs. Some programs use an asterisk, while others use a question mark. Check the program you are using to determine which rules and characters apply.

Replacement

If you have used the word "women" in your search, you will not locate a record that has the singular term "woman." However, using the wildcard character (example uses "*") by entering "wom*n" will get you both "women" and "woman."

Truncation

If you want records on a concept that is represented by a shorter root word and do not want to enter all the variations for that term, you can use a wildcard to represent all possible combinations of letters after the root term.

For example, entering "computer" will not retrieve "computers" or "computing." If you truncate the word and use the wildcard by entering "comput*" your search will retrieve "computing," and "computers" and "computation" and "compute" and all other variations of the word.

One caution with truncation is that you may retrieve records that do not match what you want to find. The example above would retrieve records on "computation of the national debt" and "computing batting averages" which may have nothing to do with computers.

PURCHASING

The purchasing function involves four steps:
1. Identifying what you wish to purchase;
2. Identifying what funds are available to make the purchase;
3. Making the purchase;
4. Verifying that the correct items are received and approving payment.

Each district has its own procedures, forms and policies for ordering materials, including library books. Some of these are based upon state or federal law and regulations, especially if you are spending state or federal funds. Other procedures are based on district policies and practices. This section will cover some general concepts and ideas.

WHAT YOU CAN DO

You are encouraged to ask your school secretary, principal, or the district library media coordinator about budgeting and purchasing policies and practices in your district.

BUDGET

It is important that you know what kinds of funds are available to support the library and how much is in the library budget. Find out what is in your library budget and record it. A sample budget form is included at the end of this chapter.

Library budgets are generally composed of two types of funds:

Categorical – these are restricted to certain specific uses or to serve specific students.

General – these are unrestricted and can be used for any purpose in the district. Most often general funds pay for salaries and operations of the district.

Sources of Funds

Funds come from different sources. Some typical sources and the kinds of funds that may be allocated for the school library are:

Federal Funds
Some districts may receive federal grants for specific purposes, such as serving disadvantaged children or bilingual programs. However, most districts receive Title VI funds which can be used for a variety of purposes. In many districts the Title VI funds are used to support their school libraries.

State Funds
Many states have funds designated for school libraries. These may be restricted for specific uses, for example, in California the School Library Fund may not be used for supplies or staffing, only for "library resources."

Some states provide funds for other general purposes, such as school improvement, reading improvement, gifted students, or student remediation. These funds are often used based on a school's plan and may be available to support the library, for example, to purchase materials or pay staffing for after school study centers or enrichment programs.

Local Funds

General Funds – The district has a great deal of discretion about how these funds are used. If the school library has paid staff, they are generally paid out of the general fund. Whether the spending decisions are made at the district level or at the individual school site is a matter of district policy.

Fundraising – In some schools, local educational foundations, Parent Teacher Associations or Home and School Clubs have supported school libraries for years, raising money for the purchase of books and computers. However, many school districts are supporting their libraries and moving away from fundraising.

WHAT YOU CAN DO

Use the form on page 117 to record all of the funds in the library budget for the year.

ORDERING

Wish List/Consideration File

It is very important that you have a system for keeping track of what you want to buy and what you have already purchased but not received. This will allow you to make the best use of the funds available and to prevent duplication of orders.

It also gives you a way of responding quickly when funds are available. Often at the end of a grant or budget year there are remaining funds that must be spent. If you can present your "wish list" quickly, you have a good chance of getting what your library needs.

There are a variety of systems for keeping track of materials you want to purchase.

Binder/File - with dividers by subject or type of material and file pages from publishers catalogs, notes or photocopies of reviews.

Database – enter relevant information that can be printed out in a variety of lists and formats for ordering materials. Keeping a database allows a quick list to be printed when funds become available unexpectedly.

Purchasing Procedures

Each district has specific procedures for submitting purchases. Check with your school secretary or principal to find out how your district does it.

Generally, the steps are:

1. Purchase requisition – this is completed with all information needed for an order and submitted for approvals.

2. Purchase Order (PO) – the PO is created by the purchasing department from the information on the requisition and sent to the vendor. Usually a copy will also be sent to the school/ department that initiated the order so you have a record of what was ordered.

RECEIVING AND PROCESSING

Receiving Materials

1. Unpack the box and find the packing slip.

2. Check off the materials received on the packing slip, verifying that you received the correct item. If an incorrect item was sent, make a note of it. It is necessary to follow up with the vendor to have the incorrect item returned and the correct item sent. Check your school's procedures to find out who is responsible for following up with the vendor. Some districts prefer to have this handled centrally, while others expect the library staff to follow up.

3. Put books in alphabetical order by author on book cart.

4. Check off each book on the purchase order, then initial and date that the items have been received.

5. Open the front cover of each book, then the back cover, continuing to open and press down a few pages at each time alternating front and back, checking as you go for damage or defects, such as pages that are missing or uncut.

6. If you find pages missing or other serious damage, note it on the purchase order and place the book aside for follow up with the vendor.

7. Send a copy of the purchase order or other confirming documents to the appropriate department so payment can be made. Check your school and district purchasing procedures for specific details.

Accession Numbers

If your school maintains an accession list (a list of all materials added to the library in the order in which they were purchased) you will need to assign an accession number to the item and note the relevant information on the accession list.

Most schools, especially those that have automated catalogs, do not maintain accession lists due to the time involved and the ability to easily get data and lists from their automated system.

Property Stamp

Every item should be stamped with a property stamp. This is a stamp that identifies the name of the library (including the district name) and the address of the library. This is very useful to get items back if they have been lost or returned in error to another library, such as the public library.

Stamp each book:
- inside the front cover;
- on the title page;
- on the back flyleaf;
- on one other page in the book – be consistent.

Your school or district might have a standard location for the property stamp, the 24th page, for example. That way, even if the front and back property stamp are obliterated or the cover is destroyed, it is easy to identify the item as belonging to your library.

Funding Stamp

Federal, state and other special sources of funds often require that materials purchased with these funds be identified by a stamp or label indicating the source of the funds and the year acquired. Though this isn't always required, it can serve as a public relations tool, graphically showing where the money came from to purchase the materials in the library.

Labels

- Spine label – attach the call number on the spine of the book at a standard height for ease of reading when on the shelf. If the spine is too narrow, attach the label to the front cover, on the left side at the same height as if on the spine.

- Property label or stamp – see above.

- Barcode – Attach the barcode to the book where it can be easily swiped and cover with barcode protector (if not already covered by clear book cover).

Location of barcode – check your school's preferred location below:
- ❑ Top right corner of back cover (horizontally or vertically)
- ❑ Top left corner of front cover
- ❑ Inside front cover
- ❑ Inside back cover

The top right on the outside back cover is used by many librarians for ease of scanning – the book doesn't need to be opened to check it out or in. Also the barcode is then on the outside edge of the book as it sits on the shelf for ease of inventory.

PROCESSING PERIODICALS

Periodicals arrive at regular intervals throughout the year. Most libraries subscribe to some periodicals, such as magazines or newspapers.

Processing procedures

Prepare a periodical check in card or sheet for each title. Library supply vendors carry preprinted periodical check in cards which are useful. Or you can create your own check-in form with the following information:
- Name of periodical.
- Frequency – how often is it published – daily, monthly, quarterly, or only during school months?
- Indicate the issue received – either year/month/day or volume/number.

It is also a good idea to note the date it was received.

A sample periodical check-in form is included on page 119 that you may duplicate and use.

Steps:

1. Check in the specific issue on the check-in form.

2. Stamp the periodical with the library property stamp on the front cover.

3. Process the periodical for check out (card, pocket, date due slip or enter into automated system and barcode it).

4. If you have a current periodicals display, remove the older issue from the magazine cover and replace with the new issue.

5. Periodically review the check-in cards to identify missing issues, those that never arrived at your library. Be sure to check the frequency – some periodicals are published irregularly, skipping certain weeks or months during the year.

6. Follow-up on missing issues by sending a claim to the publisher or periodical jobber.

Periodical Holdings

Prepare a list of all periodical subscriptions and the dates for which the library has back issues and keep it near the periodical index.

Example:

Title	Holdings
Seventeen	1995-
Teen	1995-1999
Time	1998-

If you continue to subscribe to the print edition of a magazine, do not enter a second date. If you no longer subscribe indicate the ending date of the subscription.

If you are using an electronic periodical database, you may be able to program your holdings into the database so it will automatically let students know what titles are available in your school library.

If the electronic periodical database has full text articles you may not need to keep large numbers of past issues of periodicals included in the database as students can print out the articles they need.

Remember, that you only have access to the online full text articles as long as your library maintains a subscription to the online database and so long as your computer system is working.

It is still a good idea to have some print subscriptions and to keep some back issues of popular periodicals. How many you keep depends on your student use and the space available for storage.

SCHOOL LIBRARY BUDGET

School: _____

Budget Year: _____

Source of funds	Amount	Restrictions?
Federal Funds: Title VI		
Federal Funds:		
Federal Funds:		
State Funds:		
State Funds:		
State Funds:		
Other:		
Other:		
Other:		
Other:		

Other budget information:

PERIODICAL CHECK-IN FORM

TITLE OF PERIODICAL:

FREQUENCY	NUMBER OF ISSUES	MONTHS PUBLISHED (If not year round)

ISSUES RECEIVED: Enter the year in box below. For monthly periodicals, circle the month. For weekly periodicals, write in the day of the month for the issue received under the name of the month.

YEAR _____
Jan   Feb   Mar   Apr   May   Jun   Jul   Aug   Sep   Oct   Nov   Dec

YEAR _____
Jan   Feb   Mar   Apr   May   Jun   Jul   Aug   Sep   Oct   Nov   Dec

YEAR _____
Jan   Feb   Mar   Apr   May   Jun   Jul   Aug   Sep   Oct   Nov   Dec

NOTES: List any missing issues, claims made, and other information about this periodical, such as change in publication date, title, etc. You may also enter other information on subscriptions, such as, if ordered through a jobber, a donation, etc.

FILING RULES

There are many instances when you will need to manually file items even if you have an automated system and have no catalog cards.

The rules for filing in libraries changed in 1980. If you have an older card catalog you may find that cards are filed differently, which can cause a great deal of confusion.

There are two major ways to file alphabetical items:

Word by word – files single letters or small words before a longer word beginning with the same letter.

Letter by letter – files in order by the appearance of each letter whether they are in separate words or part of a longer word.

1. Library filing rules use word by word – a single letter or small word is filed before a longer word beginning with the same letter(s).

    Example: 1. San Diego is filed before
    2. Sanders Restaurant

2. Nothing precedes something – if there is a space between words, it is filed under the first word before a longer word with no space. If the first word is the same, next file alphabetically by the second word.

    Example: 1. San Diego
    2. San Mateo
    3. Sanders Restaurant

3. If filing catalog cards and two or more entries are by the same author, next file alphabetically by the titles.

4. Disregard initial articles (a, an, the) except when used in a personal or place name.

5. Dashes, hyphens, slashes and periods are treated as if they are a blank space and separate the words.

6. Single letters or initials separated by periods, hyphens, etc., are treated as separate words. Initials without punctuation or spaces are treated as one word.

    Example: 1. U.N. Commission
    2. Under the Boardwalk
    3. UNICEF
    4. United States

7. Abbreviations are filed exactly as spelled. (This is a change from the older rules – prior to 1980 abbreviations were filed as if spelled out.)

    Example: 1. Mister Beau Jangles
    2. Mr. Smith Goes to Washington
    3. Mrs. Miniver
    4. Ms. Magazine

8. Numbers (numerals) are filed in numerical order before any letter (This is also a change from the older rules – prior to 1980 numbers were filed as if spelled out.)

Example: 1. 1 in a million
2. 66 Sunset Strip
3. One of the Best
4. Two for the road

To learn more about filing read, *ALA Filing Rules*. Chicago, IL: American Library Association, 1980.

CIRCULATION

Circulation procedures will vary according to your school and district policies.
- How often students visit the library.
- How many items they can borrow.
- What materials can be circulated.

These are all decisions that must be made in the best interests of your students and the resources available in your school library.

Manual Process

1. Remove circulation card from book, student writes in his/her name, room # and/or grade on the card.

2. Stamp date due inside book on date due slip.

3. Keep cards for checked out books in a file in some order:
   - date due;
   - author;
   - call number;
   - teacher or room number.

   The order will be determined by your needs. Often elementary students visit the library only with their class, so keeping the circulation cards in order by class or room number makes sense for easy check-in.

Automated Process

1. Keep student I.D. or barcodes in some order at circulation counter:
   - in a binder in clear baseball card sleeves, sorted by class/teacher
   - on a rolodex file alpha by last name
   - rubber banded by class, spread out on table when class comes to library.

2. Swipe or enter student code, check for holds or problems with overdues.

3. Swipe or enter barcode for item.

4. Deactivate security on item, if needed.

5. Give student date due slip.

Circulation Policies

Your circulation policies may be determined by established school or district policies.

Here are some questions that your circulation policies should answer:
- Is there a limit on the number of books that can be checked out?

- Can students check out materials if they have overdue items?

- How often will you send out overdue notices?

- How will you handle end of the year returns and clearances for students who are leaving the school?

- How will you handle reserves – requests for books that are checked out and in circulation?

- Will you charge for overdues, for lost books, damaged books?

Shelving Procedures

Books are placed on shelves in order from left to right, from top shelf to bottom shelf, then to the next shelving unit to the right, starting on the top shelf.

> Biography (92 or B) – alphabetical by the biographee, first three letters of last name.

> Fiction – alphabetical by author, then by title.

> Nonfiction – by Dewey decimal number.

> Paperbacks – fiction is filed generally alphabetically by the first letter of the author's last name. Nonfiction paperbacks are filed with other nonfiction books.

> Periodicals – alphabetically by title of publication, then in date order.

Line books up close to the front edge of the shelf.

Use bookends to keep the books standing neatly on the shelves (various types are available). Pamphlet boxes may be needed to hold slim, slippery materials.

Leave empty space on the end of each shelf so additional materials or returned materials can fit on the shelf.

Put fewer materials on the top shelves for safety and accessibility. If you have lots of shelves, leave the top shelf empty and use it for display.

Reshelving Books

1. After books have been checked in, place them on carts in shelf order, keeping fiction, nonfiction and special collections together.

2. As you shelve each book, pick it up and look it over for damage or materials left in the book, such as bookmarks, money or passes. If repairs or discard are needed, make a notation and put the book aside.

3. Check the call number and find the proper location on the shelf.

4. Place the book on the shelf and straighten the materials.

5. Check the materials to each side of the one you are reshelving to be sure they are in proper order and rearrange, if needed.

6. Continue with the next book.

Many school libraries have had automated circulation systems for several years, but some school libraries are implementing full automation for the first time including online public access catalogs.

Even if you are struggling to keep a card catalog up to date and don't think you need to know about automation, get ready now. Automating a library is an expensive task that requires a great deal of thought and planning. This section will give you some ideas and resources to help you.

Automation Checklist

Here are some questions to think about when you are investigating an automation system.

Is it an integrated system?
What modules are available?
Be sure the system is capable of handling circulation, PAC (Public Access Catalog), cataloging, and inventory functions. This should be a minimum requirement. Other modules may include serials, acquisitions, community resources, equipment booking, etc. Find out if modules can be added on later and whether new modules are in development.

Does the system use MARC records?
MARC is the standard for cataloging records in the library profession (see explanation of MARC in the next section). Make sure the system is able to export and import in either USMARC or MicroLIF MARC formats. Importing allows you to load records into your system, and exporting permits you to take your data with you when moving to a new system in the future.

How reliable is the vendor?
What support services do they offer?
How long has the vendor been in business? When you call for technical support, are you able to reach a "live" voice and get assistance? These are important questions to ask. When you are learning a new system, you need to feel comfortable about calling for help.

Is the system compatible with the network in your school or district?
If the system can't communicate with other systems on campus, you may have a hard time getting technical support or providing access from classrooms.

Does the system offer both a PC (Windows or Mac) and a Web interface?
You might not be ready now to put your catalog up on the Web, but the system you choose today should be able to grow with you.

What nearby libraries use the system?
Ask each vendor for a list of local libraries who use their system and contact them to find out if they are satisfied; what are the pros and cons, and so forth. Another way of contacting users is to join a library-related listserv such as LM_NET or your state school library listserv, if there is one.

How easy is the system to learn and navigate?

Evaluate the different modules. Are you able to go from one module to another without too much trouble; for example, edit a bibliographic record and then switch to checking out a book. Also, try to see the system from a student's point of view. Are the screens appealing and instructions clear?

School Library Automation System Vendors

There are several vendors that provide automation systems geared specifically for school libraries. This list, in alphabetical order, gives contact information for some automation vendors, including web sites where you can learn more about their products. There is no one best system, it depends on your district's needs and ability to support the system.

Auto-Graphics, Inc.
www.auto-graphics.com
3201 Temple Ave.
Pomona, CA 91768-3200
(800) 776-6939
FAX (909) 595-3506

Brodart
www.brodart.com
Library Automation Division
500 Arch St.
Williamsport, PA 17705
(800) 233-8467 x6581
FAX (570) 327-9237

CARL Corporation
www.carl.org
3801 East Florida, Suite 300
Denver, CO 80210
(888) 439-2275
FAX (303) 758-0606

Caspr, Inc.
www.caspr.com
100 Park Center Plaza, Suite 550
San Jose, CA 95113
(800) 852-2777
FAX (408) 882-0608

COMPanion
www.companioncorp.com
Library Automation Division
COMPanion Corporation
1831 Fort Union Blvd.
Salt Lake City, UT 84124
(800) 347-6439
FAX (801) 943-7752

Cuadra Associates, Inc.
www.cuadra.com
Cuadra Associates, Inc.
11835 West Olympic Blvd., Suite 855
Los Angeles, CA 90064
(310) 478-0066
FAX (310) 477-1078

Data Research Associates, Inc.
www.dra.com
1276 North Warson Rd.
St. Louis, MO 63132-1806
(800) 325-0888
FAX (314) 993-8927

Epixtech (formerly Ameritech)
www.epixtech.com
400 West 5050 North.
Provo, UT 84604-5650
(800) 288-8020
FAX (801) 223-5202

Follett Software Company
www.fsc.follett.com
1391 Corporate Drive
McHenry, IL 60050-7041
(800) 323-3397
FAX (815) 344-8774

Gateway Software Corporation

www.gscweb.com
P.O. Box 367
Fromberg, MT 59029-0367
(800) 735-3637
FAX (406) 668-7665

Gaylord Information Systems

www.gaylord.com
7272 Morgan Rd.
Liverpool, NY 13090
(800) 272-3414
FAX (315) 457-5883

Innovative Interfaces, Inc.

www.iii.com
5850 Shellmound Way
Emeryville, CA 94608
(510) 655-6200
FAX (510) 450-6350

The Library Corporation

www.tlcdelivers.com
Research Park
Inwood, WV 25428
(800) 624-0559 (Marketing)
FAX (304) 229-0295

Sagebrush Corp.

www.sagebrushcorp.com
Corporate Office
3601 Minnesota Ave.
Minneapolis, MN 55337
(800) 533-5430
FAX (952) 656-2993

SIRS Mandarin, Inc

www.sirs.com
P.O. Box 272348
Boca Raton, FL 33427-2348
(800) 232-7477
FAX (407) 994-4704

SIRSI Corporation

www.sirsi.com
101 Washington Street, S.E.
Huntsville, AL 35801-4827
(256) 704-7000
FAX (256) 704-7007

CATALOGING

Cataloging – bibliographic and physical description of an item for the collection.
Classification – a system for arranging materials according to subject or format.

Creating original cataloging and determining the classification of an item is a complicated task and best performed by professionals with training and experience. One reason that libraries are successful is because there are standards and consistency in how they operate. A book on a certain topic will be on the shelf under a certain Dewey number and four books by the same author can be located in the catalog (card or online) under that author's last name even if they are on very different subjects.

When well-meaning individuals catalog materials and classify them without having the training and experience, the library becomes less predictable and more difficult to use.

With standardized cataloging and machine readable cataloging (MARC) information, school library catalogs have information that is both accurate and complete.

MARC RECORDS

MARC stands for:
MAchine
Readable
Cataloging

The Library of Congress created LC MARC in the 1960s when it began to use computers to catalog materials. The LC MARC format evolved to become USMARC, which is the standard used by most library computer programs today. The Library of Congress maintains the USMARC format and documentation.

The MARC record codes pieces of information in a standard format, with each piece of information (called a field) assigned a number (MARC tag). Certain pieces of information, such as the author's name, are always in the same field.

This standardization means that a MARC record that is placed into several different automation systems will always have the same information in each field. These different systems have been programmed to accept the MARC record information.

See the sample MARC record located at the end of this chapter.

PRE-PROCESSING

Many schools order their books pre-processed, that is, the items come with labels, barcodes, covers, and cataloging information (either printed catalog cards or on disk). All that the school library staff needs to do is add the copy numbers, record the bar code and enter it into the catalog.

If you are ordering your materials pre-processed, be sure to carefully fill out the specification form provided by your vendor to insure that you get the exact format and type of processing you need.

Decisions about the specifications should be made district-wide so each library in the district has a similar catalog and format.

If you are not familiar with the information requested on the specifications form most vendor representatives will help you complete it.

RESOURCES

Books:

Byrne, Deborah J., *MARC Manual: Understanding and Using MARC Records.* Englewood, CO: Libraries Unlimited, 1991.

Furrie, Betty, *Understanding MARC Machine-Readable Cataloging.* Washington, DC: Library of Congress, 1998.

Sears List of Subject Headings, 17th Edition. Brooklyn, NY: H. W. Wilson, 2000.

Zuiderveld, Sharon, editor, *Cataloging Correctly for Kids, 3rd edition.* Chicago, IL: American Library Association, 1998.

SAMPLE MARC RECORD

Sample MARC Record

Leader	01041cam 2200265 a 4500
Control No	001 ###89048230 /AC/r91
Control No. ID	003 DLC
DTLT	005 19911106082810.9
Fixed Data	008 891101s1990 maua j 001 0 eng
LCCN	010 ## $a ###89048230 /AC/r91
ISBN	020 ## $a 0316107514 :
	$c $12.95
ISBN	020 ## $a 0316107506 (pbk.) :
	$c $5.95 ($6.95 Can.)
Cat. Source	040 ## $a DLC
	$c DLC
	$d DLC
LC Call No.	050 00 $a GV943.25
	$b .B74 1990
Dewey No.	082 00 $a 796.334/2
	$2 20
ME:Pers Name	100 1# $a Brenner, Richard J.,
	$d 1941-
Title	245 10 $a Make the team.
	$p Soccer :
	$b a heads up guide to super soccer! /
	$c Richard J. Brenner.
Variant Title	246 30 $a Heads up guide to super soccer
Edition	250 ## $a 1st ed.
Publication	260 ## $a Boston :
	$b Little, Brown,
	$c c1990.
Phys Desc	300 ## $a 127 p. :
	$b ill. ;
	$c 19 cm.
Note: General	500 ## $a "A Sports illustrated for kids book."
Note: Summary	520 ## $a Instructions for improving soccer skills. Discusses dribbling, heading, playmaking, defense, conditioning, mental attitude, how to handle problems with coaches, parents, and other players, and the history of soccer.
Subj: Topical	650 #0 $a Soccer
	$v Juvenile literature.
Subj: Topical	650 #1 $a Soccer.

Sample of a brief record display as seen by a patron:

TITLE :   Make the team. Soccer : a heads up guide to super soccer! / J. Brenner.
AUTHOR :   Brenner, Richard J.
PUBLISHED :   Little, Brown, c1990.
MATERIAL :   127 p.

Copies Available :   796.334 Bre

Sample of a full record display as seen by a patron:

TITLE :   Make the team. Soccer : a heads up guide to super soccer! / Richard J. Brenner.
ADDED TITLE :   Heads up guide to super soccer
AUTHOR :   Brenner, Richard J., 1941-
PUBLISHED :   1st ed. Boston : Little, Brown, c1990.
MATERIAL :   127 p. : ill. ; 19 cm.
NOTE :   "A Sports Illustrated for kids book."
NOTE :   Instructions for improving soccer skills. Discusses heading, playmaking, defense, conditioning, mental attitude, how to handle problems with coaches, parents, and other players, and the history of soccer.
SUBJECT :   Soccer—Juvenile literature.
                   Soccer.

Copies Available :   796.334 Bre

Sample of a catalog card:

796.334   Brenner, Richard J., 1941-25
Bre   Make the team. Soccer : a heads up guide to super
           soccer! / Richard J. Brenner. — 1st ed. — Boston : Little,
           Brown, c1990.

   127 p. : ill. ; 19 cm.

       "A Sports Illustrated for kids book."
       Summary: Instructions for improving soccer skills. Discusses dribbling, heading,
       playmaking, defense, conditioning, mental attitude, how to handle problems with
       coaches, parents, and other players, and the history of soccer.

   ISBN 0316107514 : $12.95

     1. Soccer — Juvenile literature. 2. Soccer. II. Title: Heads up guide to super soccer. II. Title.

                                                                    89-48230/AC/r91
                                                                    MARC

Glossary of Library Terms

This glossary includes library, technology and educational terms. Many of the terms appear in the content of this Handbook, but this glossary includes additional words that you might encounter working in school libraries.

AACR II
Anglo-American cataloging rules. General rules for entries and descriptive cataloging.

AASL
American Association of School Librarians

Abridged
A condensed or edited version of a longer work, for example, an abridged dictionary.

Abstract
A brief, non-judgmental summary of a work, often of a periodical article, accompanied by the bibliographic description of the work.

Acceptable use policy
A school board approved document outlining policies and procedures regarding student and staff use of the Internet and other online services.

Accession number
An identifying number assigned to an item in the order that the resource is acquired.

Acquisitions
Materials which are purchased for the library, or the department or staff person responsible for purchasing materials.

ALA
American Library Association

Annotated bibliography
A bibliography in which each citation is followed by an annotation containing a brief description and/or evaluative summary, synopsis, or abstract.

Annual
A yearly publication.

Archives
Public records or historical documents, or the place where such records and documents are kept.

Art print
Printed reproduction of a work of art.

ASCII
American Standard Code for Information Interchange. ASCII (pronounced "as-key") is a binary code used to store date and transmit data between computers and computer peripherals.

Atlas
A book of maps and sometimes other information, such as statistical data, tables, charts, glossaries, or pronunciation guides.

Audiocassette
Magnetic audiotape on which sound has been recorded, contained in a cartridge.

Audiovisual materials
Non-book materials such as filmstrips, videotapes, recordings, films, records, CDs, etc. Sometimes these are just called "AV." See also Non-print Materials.

Author
The writer; the person or body chiefly responsible for the intellectual content of any given written, filmed or recorded work.

Author card
A catalog card with an author entry on the first or top line, which includes the author's last name, first name, and middle name or initial.

Authority control
Use of a Controlled Vocabulary to catalog materials for library. Subject headings, author names, corporate names, and series are all fields governed by authority control.

Autobiography
The life story of a person, actually written by that person.

Barcode
A defined pattern of alternating parallel bars and spaces, representing numbers and other characters, that are machine readable. Usually available on labels and placed on circulating items so that they can be checked out and inventoried using a barwand.

Bibliographic citation
The information needed for someone to find an item. For example the citation for a book would include the Title, Author or Editor, Place of Publication, Publisher, and Year of Publication. A citation for an article would contain the Author, Title of the Article, Title of the Periodical, Volume Number, Issue Number (or sometimes the month and date), and the Page Numbers.

Bibliographic record
In a database, information about one item is stored as a "record." Records are made up of several fields, such as the title, author, and publisher.

Bibliography
A list of items such as books, documents, articles, videos, etc. arranged in a logical order and having something in common such as the author or producer, a subject, or a geographic region.

Big6 Skills Approach to Information Problem Solving
An information literacy curriculum, an information problem-solving process, and a set of skills which provide a strategy for effectively and efficiently meeting information needs.

Biography
The life story of a person.

BIP
Books in Print. A comprehensive listing of all books currently in print. Author and title volumes are available. Listings by subject are found in Subject Guide to Books in Print.

Block scheduling
The manipulation of time periods to better meet the educational and emotional needs of both students and teachers.

Book pocket
A paper pocket glued in the book or on the audiovisual container to hold the circulation or date due card.

Book return
A place to return books borrowed from the library. Book return slots are usually near the circulation counter in the library and outside the library near the main entrance.

Book truck
A cart used to hold books before they are reshelved, and then used to carry the books to the shelves for re-shelving.

Bookmark
A feature available in some browsers, such as Netscape, that enables you to quickly go to an Internet address without having to type

the address. A short cut method to access Internet resources.

Boolean operators
Used to narrow or broaden a reference search:
AND requires that both or all words appear;
OR searches for either term;
NOT eliminates the term.

Bound
A term referring to pages, sheets or issues of periodicals which have been covered with binding, usually hardback, to create a single volume. This process is used in libraries to preserve items for long-term use.

Caldecott Medal
An award presented each year by the American Library Association to an American illustrator for the most distinguished picture book for children published during the previous year.

Call number
Letters, numbers, and symbols (used separately or in combination) assigned to a book to show its location in the library shelving system. Call numbers are derived from the classification system used by the particular library, e.g., Dewey Decimal System or Library of Congress.

Card catalog
An index to the materials in the library, composed of a file of cards representing the author, title, and subjects of books or other materials. The cabinet in which the cards are filed.

Catalog
A list of items such as books, periodicals, maps and/or videos arranged in a defined order. The list usually records, describes and indexes the resources of a collection, a library, or a group of libraries.

Cataloging
Bibliographic and physical description of an item for the collection. Includes author, title, subject headings, and imprint followed by the collation and further description.

CD-ROM
An abbreviation for the term "Compact Disc-Read Only Memory." A read-only disk used to store printed information such as periodical indexes.

Centralized acquisitions
The purchase of materials, supplies and equipment for the collections of all the schools in a system carried out from a central source.

Centralized cataloging
Bibliographic records and descriptions of the items in the collections of all the schools in the system carried out from a central source.

Centralized processing services
Preparation of all materials and equipment for circulation for each school in the system carried out from a central source.

Certification
A State Department of Education endorsed document serving as evidence for the holder to work in a specified field of education.

CIP
Cataloging in Publication. Cataloging data found on the Verso page of many books. Produced by the Library of Congress.

Circulation
1. The tasks that comprise the distribution, tracking, and retrieval of the library collection. 2. The total number of volumes

lent during a given period of use outside the library.

Citation
See Bibliographic Citation

Claimed
Notification that a periodical was not received as expected.

Classification
Any of various systems for arranging books and other materials according to subject or format; the subject arrangement of knowledge. See also: Dewey Decimal Classification System or Library of Congress Classification System.

Collation
In cataloging, the physical description of a bibliographic item (book, tape, film) which appears on the line following the imprint.

Collection
All print and nonprint materials and equipment that comprise the holdings of the library.

Collection development
Activities related to building, maintaining, evaluating, and expanding library collections—includes user needs assessment, budget management, selection policy formation, resource sharing, and weeding.

Collection map
A tool for assessing the total number of books, the number of books per student, and the strengths and weaknesses of the collection in relation to instructional priorities.

Collective biography
A book about the lives of persons who have at least one characteristic in common. Classified with the number 920 in Dewey Decimal System.

Computer software
The computer programs (usually on disks) that are used for programming and applications such as word processing, databases, spreadsheets, simulations, and computer-assisted instruction.

Controlled vocabulary
The words and phrases used by a subject specialist when creating subject headings for an article, book, and so forth, for a specific index or catalog.

Copyright
Legislation applicable to the rights of authors and producers of print and nonprint materials governing others' use of such items. Provides protection against unlawful copying for a specified number of years.

Coretta Scott King Award
The Coretta Scott King Award is presented to authors and illustrators of African descent whose distinguished books promote an understanding and appreciation of the "American Dream."

Corporate Entry
A catalog or index entry under the name of an organization or institution, rather than under an individual name.

Cross reference
Many catalogs and indexes have "See" or "See Also" references that refer you to the correct heading or to a related heading on your subject.

Cumulative index
An index in which several previously published indexes are combined into one book. Usually covers several months or years.

Cutter number
An alpha-numeric scheme used for indication of the author or main entry following the classification number. Its purpose is as a filing device to alphabetize or arrange main entries within a given classification number.

Database
A collection of computer records that have a standard format, usually containing fields that are searchable and allow some electronic manipulation such as sorting or grouping.

DDC
See Dewey Decimal Classification.

Depository
A library which automatically receives all publications published by a governmental entity; e.g. Superintendent of Documents, state department, United Nations, and so forth.

Descriptors
Words or phrases used as Subject Headings.

Dewey Decimal Classification
A classification system designed for organizing nonfiction materials. Used mostly by public and school libraries.

Dictionary
A book which defines the terms of a language, profession, discipline, or specialized area of knowledge. The terms are arranged in alphabetical order.

Domain
The Internet is set up hierarchically and the domain is the last part of the address which describes the type of site it is. Examples:
    .com = commercial

    .edu = educational
    .gov = governmental
    .org = organization

Download
To move a copy of a file from a multi-user system or server to your microcomputer.

Due date
Date by which an item must be returned.

Edition
All copies of a book printed at any time from the same setting of type.

Encyclopedia
A work containing factual articles on subjects in every field of knowledge, usually arranged alphabetically.

FAQ
Frequently Asked Questions. Throughout the Internet FAQs are listed which contain questions and answers to frequently asked questions. They are found on web pages, FTP sites, and Usenet groups.

Fiction
Literature about events that did not actually take place. Genres include historical fiction, mysteries, romance, suspense, science fiction, westerns, and so forth.

Field
A subdivision of the computer record used for a defined category or purpose. For example in a bibliographic record is the author field, where the author's name is located.

Field limiting
Requiring that a keyword or phrase appear in a specific field when conducting an online and/or database search. See also Limit.

Field specific search

A search of a database that identifies the occurrence of a term, using either free text or controlled vocabulary, in a particular Field in the database. A field specific search is more precise than searching all fields. A common example is a "subject" search in a library catalog.

Filmstrip

A series of still pictures with or without captions in sequential order on 35mm film.

Fixed scheduling

Each class is scheduled to visit the library on a certain day and time and does not have the opportunity to use the library at other times.

Flexible scheduling

Provides opportunities for students and classes to use the library as the need arises rather than having a fixed schedule with a regular day and time to visit the library.

Flyleaf

The first and last page of a book, usually blank.

Folio

Oversized books that are too big to fit on regular shelves. Usually kept in separate area on shelving spaced for taller books.

Free text

Usually describes a method of searching a database using natural language rather than a controlled vocabulary. The person searching would search as many terms as he could think of that would be related to the topic of interest. The computer would search all fields or designated fields.

Full text

Some computer databases only include citations of articles or documents, while others may provide the complete or full text of the item.

Full-text searching

Searching all or most of the words in a document; approach likely to result in many hits; best used when searching for unusual terms or combinations of terms.

Government documents

Monographs, serial publications, reports, or official communication published by any governing body—federal, state, county, or municipal.

Hard copy

The actual physical paper copy of a book, magazine, or other source, as opposed to its online or microform equivalent.

Hardware

Audiovisual and computer equipment.

Hit

A document relevant to your research.

Hold

See Reserve.

Holdings

The list of copies of a book, or other items in the catalog, showing which libraries own the item and whether or not it is available to be checked out.

HTML

Hypertext Markup Language, or the language in which Web documents are written.

Icon

A small picture or symbol representing a computer program, file, or feature.

Index

A list, in alphabetical or numerical order, of the topics, names, etc., that are treated or mentioned in a publication or group of publications, along with references to the pages where the topics are discussed. Author, subject, and title indexes are common; the type of index depends on the type of material covered in the publication.

Instructional technology specialist

A new certification under educational reform which requires competency in the use of productivity tools; in evaluation and selection of computer based curriculum materials; in integration of those materials into the curriculum; in the use of at least one programming language; and a knowledge of the ethical, legal and human issues of technology as they relate to education and society.

Interactive video

Video programs in which the user controls the learning process by choosing from various options presented in a video program that is interfaced with a computer.

Interlibrary loan (ILL)

A process that permits library materials and resources to be borrowed or shared between two libraries that are not under the same governing or funding authority.

Internet

A huge, worldwide network of millions of computers and computer files. The best known portion of it is the World Wide Web, but it also includes e-mail, chat groups, etc. To connect to the Internet you need a computer with an Internet connection and software (a browser such as Netscape or Internet Explorer) which allows you to view the files available.

Internet filters

Software that does any of the following: block access to Internet sites listed in an internal database of the product; block access to Internet sites listed in a database maintained external to the product itself; or scan the contents of Internet sites which a user seeks to view and block access based on the occurrence of certain words or phrases on those sites. Products currently on the market include Bess, CyberPatrol, I-Gear, SurfWatch, WebSense, WebManager, and X-Stop.

Inventory

The process of checking every item in the library manually against the shelf list or electronically against the holdings in the online catalog system.

ISBD

International Standard Bibliographic Description. Represents a set of standards for the creation of bibliographic records that includes both content specifications and formatting requirements for library automation.

ISBN

International Standard Book Number. A unique, mathematically-generated, 10-digit number assigned to a book. Provides information about the publisher and is usually located on the Verso of the book.

ISSN

International Standard Serial Number

Journal

A periodical on a specialized topic. Journals are often published by a professional association, society, foundation, or institute. A referreed journal is one in which the process to determine if the article will be accepted for publication is done by professional colleagues or peers (also known as the peer review process). Sometimes these periodicals are also called scholarly journals. See also Magazine.

Keyword searching
Searching which uses a few key, or important, words to retrieve books or articles on a specific topic or associated with those words in some way. The keywords could be used to search from the text of the document (if it is a full-text database) or some named field (author, title, etc.) depending on the database being used and the searcher's intent. Often used for very new topics for which controlled vocabulary indexes will not have a subject term yet established.

Kit
A collection of media designed to be used as a unit.

LC
See Library of Congress Classification System.

LCCN
Library of Congress Catalog Number. A number assigned by the Library of Congress to books they catalog. Consists of the date cataloged followed by an accession number. Usually found on the Verso of a book.

Lexile
The Lexile Framework, developed by MetaMetrics, is a tool that makes it possible to place readers and text on the same scale. The difference between a reader's Lexile measure and a text's Lexile measure is used to forecast the comprehension the reader will have with the text.

Library of Congress Classification System
A classification system developed by the Library of Congress for its collection. Used mostly by academic and special libraries.

Limit
A term/function that allows the results of a search to be narrowed further by limiting to specific criteria such as location, date, or type of material.

Loan period
The length of time library materials may be checked out.

Magazine
A periodical containing news stories or articles on various subjects and written for general readership (as opposed to a scholarly or technical audience.) See Also Journal.

Main entry card
The catalog card which contains all of the information necessary to identify a work. Usually this is the author card. Where there is no identifiable author, or for audiovisual resources, the title card is used as the main entry. Used in card catalog systems.

Manuscript
A handwritten or typed composition, rather than printed.

Map
A drawing or representation of a geographic area.

MARC
Machine Readable Cataloging. An industry-wide standard for making and storing bibliographic records so that they can be shared by and accessible from different library automation programs. Terms

associated with MARC records include: fields, tags, subfields, subfield codes, indicators, and content designators.

Meta-Search Engine
In a meta-search engine, you submit keywords in its search box, and it transmits your search simultaneously to several individual search engines and their databases of web pages. Within a few seconds, you get back results from all the search engines queried. (Examples: Profusion, Dogpile, Mamma, Metacrawler).

Microfiche
A small, flat sheet, usually 4 x 6 or 3 x 5 inches, of photographic film which contains micro images arranged in horizontal or vertical rows.

Microfilm
Photographic film showing micro images of publications, such as the contents of journals and newspapers.

Microform
Refers to material (reports, articles, books, documents, etc.) recorded on photographic film at a greatly reduced size. Examples include microfilm and microfiche.

MicroLIF
Microcomputer Library Interchange Format. A means of communicating or loading MARC data into microcomputer-based automation systems. MicroLIF was developed so that book and data vendors could supply complete MARC data to their customers on disk in a format that could be easily loaded into a microcomputer-based circulation or online catalog system.

Model
A three-dimensional representation of an object reproduced in the size of the original or to scale.

Modem
A device that allows a computer to talk, send, and receive information from or to another computer over telephone lines. Derived from the words modulator demodulator.

Monograph
A scholarly book on a single subject, class of subjects, or person. Within the library field, this term is often used for any non-serial publication.

Motion picture
A length of film, with or without recorded sound, bearing a sequence of images that creates the illusion of movement when projected in rapid succession.

Natural language
When choosing words or phrases to describe a document, article, book or other material's subject content, the indexer (individual creating an index) can select any appropriate term often using language from the document itself. Compare with controlled vocabulary.

Networking
The use of resources outside the school library media center to provide needed information; such sources may include public, academic, or special libraries, community organizations and businesses, shared databases, and human resources.

Networks
A system whereby various computer terminals and/or peripherals are interconnected by wire and other electronic means, either as local area networks (LAN) or wide area networks (WAN).

Newbery Medal
An award presented each year by the American Library Association to an American author for a distinguished contribution to literature for children.

Non-circulating
This designation is used for materials that cannot be checked out, such as reference books.

Nonfiction
Literature that describes things or events that actually happened or are supposed to be true.

Nonprint
Any library material that is not printed on paper. This would include videos, compact discs, or microfilm. See also audiovisual materials.

OCLC
Ohio College Library Center. A library processing center which has a data base built on the holdings of its constituent libraries and MARC records. Cataloging data is received online, and upon command, catalog cards are produced. Also acts as a union catalog by giving locations of libraries holding any given title.

Online
The ability to use a computer, modem, and telephone line and/or radio frequency cable to access information outside the school library media center.

Online catalog
A catalog in electronic (machine-readable) format and able to be accessed online. Also known as an OPAC (Online Public Access Catalog).

OPAC
See Online Catalog.

Overdue
An item that has not been returned by its due date.

Overdue notice
A reminder sent to a patron to return items after the due date has passed.

Periodical
A publication that is produced at regular intervals, or "periodically" under the same title and is intended to appear indefinitely. Generally the frequency is more often than annually, such as weekly, monthly, quarterly, and so forth.

Periodical Holdings List
An alphabetical list of periodicals owned by a library indicating which years of the periodical the library owns and where they are located.

Periodical index
A subject, author or title Index to a group of periodicals. Examples include the Reader's Guide to Periodical Literature, ERIC, and so forth.

Portal (Internet sites)
An Internet site that aims to be a "one stop" resource for its users. Each site contains such services as e-mail, chat rooms, shopping opportunities, news, weather, stock quotes, search engines and directories, and other links.

Print resources
Books, periodicals, and newspapers in the school library media collection.

Rack
Shelf or shelves used for displaying books or other library materials.

Readability formulas
Devices, indexes, or methods for determining the level of difficulty of written material based on the vocabulary, sentence length and structure, and other factors.

Reader's advisory services
Activities performed by library staff to bring books and readers together. These activities may include providing book recommendations, preparing bibliographies of related works or web sites, arranging for author visits, and so forth.

Ready reference
Reference books other than abstracts, bibliographies, or indexes used for quick information requiring a single, simple answer.

Realia
Real objects or specimens.

Record
See Bibliographic Record.

Reference books
Used to look up brief information on subjects, unlike the kind of book you'd read from cover to cover. Examples include dictionaries, encyclopedias, atlases, almanacs, and so forth. Usually noncirculating.

Reference service
The aid given by library staff to a library user to find information. The extent and level of service given varies according to the question and its complexity.

Remote access
The use of computer files via input/output devices connected electronically to a computer.

Renew
The procedure for re-checking out a book to extend the loan period.

Reprint
Either: 1) a book that has been printed or reproduced at a later date than the original printing but using the same type and the same content; or 2) a periodical article or a chapter from a book which is issued separately from the larger publication at a later date.

Reserve
A hold placed on something in the library's collection that is checked out to someone else. When the item is returned, the computer notifies the library staff that someone is waiting for it so it can be set aside.

Resource sharing
Personnel, facilities, equipment, materials, and other resources and services shared among persons and/or organizations.

Retrospective conversion
The process of turning a library's existing catalog into machine-readable form. While the process usually involves the conversion of shelf list cards, existing machine-readable records can also be converted. Retrospective conversion can be accomplished in several ways, and the best method(s) for your library depends on collection type and size, budget, quality demands, time constraints, and staff needs.

School library media center
The place in a school where a centralized collection of selected, organized, and managed resources are available for teaching and learning.

School library media program
A systematic plan for teaching the skills needed to access, use, interpret, evaluate, and apply the information, resources and ideas that are available in the school library media center.

Search
Using a database to look for information. The commands or words you type in are referred to as a "search."

Search engine
Allows users to search a database of web sites by using keywords or phrases. (Examples: Infoseek, Hot Bot, Excite, Alta Vista, Lycos, Yahoo.)

See Also reference
A direction on a catalog card or computer screen which redirects the user from a name or term used to other names or terms which are related to it. See Cross Reference.

See reference
A direction on a catalog card or computer screen which redirects the user from a name or term which is not used to names or terms which are used. See Cross Reference.

Selection policy
A written document, developed in cooperation with representatives from the school community, that sets forth the criteria used to choose materials for the school library media center collection.

Serial
Any publication issued in successive parts, appearing at intervals, usually regular ones, and as a rule, intended to be continued indefinitely. The term includes periodicals, newspapers, annuals, numbered monographic series, and the proceedings and transactions of organizations or societies.

Series
A succession of volumes, issues, or media published with related subjects or authors, similar in format and price, or continuous numbering.

Shelf list
A card file which is the inventory of all the books and other resources in the library collection arranged in the same order as the resources are located on the shelf.

Shelving
Collectively, the shelves upon which books and other library materials are stored. See also Rack, Stack.

Slide
A single frame of 35mm film in a mounting, usually 2 inches x 2 inches.

Sound filmstrip
A series of still pictures with or without captions in sequential order on 35mm film, accompanied by a sound track.

Sound slide
A single frame of 35mm film in a mounting, usually 2 inches x 2 inches, accompanied by sound.

Spine label
A label located at the bottom of a book's spine. Indicates where a book should be shelved in the library.

Stacks
The shelves or bookcases on which the library's materials are stored.

Standing order

An order placed to receive all parts of a work as published such as multi-volume works, reference books, series, serials, and so forth, until a publisher or dealer is otherwise notified.

Style manual
Special handbooks that illustrate the accepted forms for citing references in bibliographies, footnotes, and endnotes. Some style manuals are for general use. Others are published by professional associations as format guides for articles in journals in that field of knowledge and research.

Subject card
A catalog card which has the subject of the item on the top line printed in capital letters. Used in card catalog system.

Subject headings
The word or phrase used to describe the subject content of a work. Also known as descriptors. A controlled vocabulary, such as Sears Subject Headings or Library of Congress Subject Headings, is most often used.

Superintendent of Documents Classification System
A system of arranging federal government publications in an alpha/numerical order based on the name of the major issuing governmental department (such as Education Dept, Commerce Dept, etc.). Often referred to as the SuDoc Classification System.

Support staff
The clerical and technical assistants who work with the school library media specialist in operating the school library media center.

Technical services
Functions concerned with the acquisition, cataloging, and classification of library materials and preparation of library materials for use by students and staff.

Technology
The electronic resources and techniques that may provide or assist in the creation, display, organization, and retrieval of information.

Thesaurus
1. A reference work of synonyms, words with similar meanings. 2. When an index or database uses controlled vocabulary, the thesaurus is an alphabetical listing of the terms currently in use. The thesaurus will also show relationships between terms such as synonymous or related terms, hierarchical arrangements (broader terms, narrower terms), and provide references from terms not currently in use to acceptable terms.

Title card
A catalog card that has the title of an item printed on the top line. Used in card catalog system.

Title Page
A page near the beginning of a book on which is printed the official title of the book and, usually, the author, publisher, and the place and date of publication. The information on the title page is used to prepare the main entry of bibliographic record.

Tracings
A record of the subject and added entries made for the work, usually listed on the bottom or end of the main entry card.

Truncation

Searching using a word root plus any suffixes that may occur with it. This involves typing the word root along with a special symbol, which can vary from one database to another. For example, "REFORM*" would find "reform," "reforms," "reformer," "reformation," and so forth.

Unabridged
A complete work that is printed just as the author intended without any deletions or other changes.

Union catalog
A catalog showing the holdings of a given group of libraries. The OCLC data base qualifies as a union catalog since it indicates libraries which hold any given title.

Union list
A list of materials, in a designated format or on a designated subject, that are available in a group of libraries; such as, A Union List of Serials or Microforms.

URL
Uniform Resource Locator, an Internet address of a web site usually beginning with "http://"

Vendors
Companies that market books, equipment, supplies, and other items.

Verso
The back of the title page.

Vertical file
A collection of pamphlets, newspaper clippings, or other small published items usually stored in a file cabinet.

Videocassette
Electromagnetic tape on which pictures and sound have been recorded, contained in a cartridge and designed for playback using a videocassette player and television.

Videodisc
A disc that contains high-quality audio and visual data optically encoded into a metallic surface. Played by using a videodisc player which can be linked to a computer and/or television monitor.

Volume
This word is used to describe two different materials: 1) a series of printed sheets, bound, typically in book form. 2) an arbitrary number of consecutive issues of a periodical.

Weeding
Re-evaluating and removing obsolete materials from the collection.

Wildcard
In searching, entering a character (usually a question mark or an asterisk) that tells the computer to "accept anything in this position." For example the entry of "wom?n" when searching a title might find all titles that have the word "women" and "woman" in them.

INDEX

FEEDBACK FORM

We want to be sure this Handbook meets the needs of school library staff. Your comments will help us to improve future editions. We would appreciate it if you would please take a few minutes to complete this form and send or FAX to:

Linworth Publishing, Inc.
480 E. Wilson Bridge Road, Suite L
Worthington, OH 43085-2372
FAX: 614-436-9490

Name (optional):

School/District:

Please circle the phrase that best describes your answer to the following questions:

1. I found the information: very useful   somewhat useful   not useful

2. The amount of information was: too much   just right   too little

3. I found the Handbook: easy to use   difficult to use

4. The Handbook format was: clear   confusing

Please comment on the following questions:

5. I wish the following information had been included in the Handbook:

6. Give an example of how you have used the Handbook in your job:

7. How would you rate the Handbook: 1   2   3   4   5   6   7   8   9   10
            (1 = very poor and 10 = excellent)

8. Any other comments?

Thank you for taking the time to complete this Feedback form!

Please fold, insert into an envelope, stamp and mail to:

Linworth Publishing, Inc.
480 E. Wilson Bridge Road, Suite L
Worthington, OH 43085-2372